Thelma,
Thank you for helping
me celebrate!

Valerie Shantz

SHORT Spells

Scenes & Monologues

sandra dempsey
marty chan
eugene stickland
barbara sapergia
brad fraser

Short Spells Scenes & Monologues © Copyright 1998 Valerie Shantz
Playwrights Canada Press
54 Wolseley St., 2nd fl. Toronto, Ontario CANADA M5T 1A5
Tel: (416) 703-0201 Fax: (416) 703-0059
e-mail: cdplays@interlog.com   http://www.puc.ca

Playwrights Canada Press publishes with the generous assistance of The Canada Council for the Arts - Writing and Publishing Section and the Ontario Arts Council.
Thanks to Coteau Books, Scirocco Drama, and NeWest Press for permission to excerpt selections from their publications.

Cover painting by Shawn Skeir.

Canadian Cataloguing in Publication Data
Main entry under title:
        Short spells : scenes & monologues
ISBN 0-88754-559-9
I. Monologues, Canadian (English).* 2. Canadian drama (English) - 20th century.* I. Shantz, Valerie.
PS8315.S63 1998   C812'.04508054 C98-932166-5
PR9196.6.S63 1998

First edition: October, 1998.
Printed and bound in Winnipeg, Manitoba, Canada.

Valerie Shantz is a Winnipeg-based writer, dramaturg and independant academic. She is the former director of the Saskatoon Fringe Festival and was a playwright in residence at Edmonton's Northern Light Theatre for the 1996/97 and 1997/98 seasons. As a dramaturg she has worked with writers from Winnipeg, Edmonton, Whitehorse and Juneau, Alaska. Her critical writing has been published in *Canadian Theatre Review* and *Australasian Drama Studies*.

Introduction

In 1987 I met my first 'Prairie Playwright' in the form of Bruce McManus who had been brought to my Winnipeg high school as part of the Artists in the Schools program. He read from his play "Caffe", a piece originally written for the University of Winnipeg graduating acting class. Until then I was unaware of Canadian playwrighting and oblivious to its existence in my home city. Bruce's reading was my introduction to the notion that not only were there Canadian playwrights, but they were living and working around me; that to be a writer did not only mean novels, poetry or short stories, but plays. Writing plays wasn't just something that happened far away.

A year later I attended the inaugural year of the Winnipeg Fringe Festival and found a community of people living and working in theatre. I now understood that Bruce was not the only playwright in Winnipeg; that this was something that people did, that I could do. That it was an option at all.

The Fringe Festivals proved to be a significant opportunity for new writers, and a significant showcase for many of the playwrights included in this collection. Brad Fraser, Yvette Nolan, Harry Rintoul, Bettina Grassmann, Ian Ross, Marty Chan and David Belke have all 'cut their teeth' on the three prairie Fringe Festivals (Winnipeg, Saskatoon and Edmonton). At the same time I have became increasingly involved. I began to coordinate Fringe Festivals, working at both Winnipeg and Saskatoon, and then began to work as a dramaturg. Through this, I am exposed to a great deal of the theatrical work happening in these and other western communities. For the playwright in the prairies, geography dictates that word of mouth is often confined to local circles, or if there is broader interest, it is rare for Artistic Directors and others to travel to see the show in its home community. In working across the prairies, I have been struck by how often local writers with solid productions under them are not known outside of their home communities.

What I read about prairie theatre was of 'kitchen sink dramas' and documentary style pieces; as an audience member I saw a great deal more. When Playwrights Canada Press approached me to edit this collection I knew that the work was out there; the challenge would be to gather it together. I was interested in compiling a collection which demonstrated the diversity of theatrical work I was seeing. However, in inviting submissions, I faced an interesting conundrum.

During the process of talking with writers and collecting submissions I was struck by the number of playwrights who did not feel that they had anything to offer to a collection of prairie plays as they did not consider themselves to be 'Prairie Playwrights.' Most of the playwrighting happening in the prairie provinces right now is out of urban centres. The traditional view of prairie plays as kitchen sink dramas or documentary theatre, predominantly about rural or small town experience, left many writers counting themselves out. They must have been reading the same books and articles as me. Does that mean that if you don't write about being in the middle of the prairie, you aren't a prairie writer? There are plays in this collection that do reflect this experience, Joanna McClelland Glass' "Play Memory" and Barbara Sapergia's "Roundup" being two examples, but stand in downtown Winnipeg or Edmonton and 'prairie' may be one of the last words that comes to mind.

Fortunately, word got out and what results is a collection that I hope reflects the diversity of style and content in approach to theatre occurring on stages in Manitoba, Saskatchewan and Alberta.

This is one of the reasons why this kind of book is important. It is for those readers who are not familiar with plays from the prairie provinces of Canada, as well as for those of us who, as prairie writers, need to begin to see ourselves as belonging here; that to be a prairie writer does not prescribe a theatrical style or content, but a merely a place of beginning.

A case in point is Mansel Robinson's "Downsizing Democracy: A Polemic". Robinson's piece is fiercely political and walks the fine line between lecture and performance — casting its audience as invested characters. It takes its home — the prairies — as its starting point, but uses that home audience to comment on the country's affairs. Similarly, "Elephant Wake", by Jonathan Christenson and Joey Tremblay uses a tiny Saskatchewan town as its backdrop, but effectively take advantage of that particular understanding of place to say much more about loss of culture and home. Bruce McManus' "Selkirk Avenue", a Winnipeg contemporary classic, derives its understanding of place through its inhabitants — introducing us to the Winnipeg street through its characters. As they are transformed by the years, so is our understanding of the place of which he writes.

There are also several pieces about characters in exile. Whether it be Maureen Hunter's "Atlantis", David Belke's "Maltese Bodkin", or Yvette Nolan's "Annie Mae's Movement", the understanding of place is drawn in terms of absence.

This is not to say that everyone is writing about an understanding of location. The concerns of these writers spans much more than that. There are several decidedly 'queer' plays excerpted here. Brad Fraser, Harry Rintoul, and Brian Drader contribute three visions of gay life on the prairies. I'm also pleased to be able to publish a section of "fareWel", Ian Ross' Governor General's Literary Award winning play. It and Nolan's "Annie Mae's Movement" are testament to strong writing in and of itself and to a growing First Nations presence amongst prairie writers. Sandra Dempsey, Marty Chan, David Belke, and Padma Viswanathan contribute their own quirky texts.

Stylistically, these pieces demand diverse approach. Where Kit Brennan's "Magpie" incorporates the use of dance, Shawna Dempsey and Lorri Millan's "Plastic Bride" uses its distinct costume to contrast with the text, giving it an heightened theatricality.

Perhaps it is through these dissimilar approaches, the uncommon visions, that we get a true sense of what prairie writing is: diverse and challenging. Writers from the Prairies are more than just transplanted central Canadians; their writing is of this place, however surprising that place may seem to be.

As Connie Gault's character says in "Otherwise Bob" in examining his proposition of crumbled tin foil reopened "We've agreed have we? That the lines are random? They go all over the place? There's no pattern to them." I invite you to approach this collection similarly. Let us agree on their seeming randomness but with the same question of what the useful patterns may be.

Valerie Shantz

Editors Note: My thanks to Angela Rebeiro, Tony Hamill and Yvette Nolan for their assistance with the creation of this book.

SHORT Spells

Otherwise Bob

by Connie Gault

"Otherwise Bob" is the inversion of Jennifer's life. First she visits his home, then he comes to hers; in both locations he has the same effect, whatever persona she presents, he turns her inside out. This scene takes place at Bob's home, which also houses his bookstore; his parents, Albert and Marie, are present, though Marie sits like a statue throughout the experiment.

Scene in which BOB tries to convince JENNIFER that goodness is a viable theory.

The light dims to near darkness.

BOB	Ladies and gentlemen —
JENNIFER	— Gentleman. There's only one. Even that is highly dubious.
ALBERT	I wonder if I've been offended?
BOB	Ladies and gentleman —
ALBERT	— Excuse me? I'd like to know if I've been offended.
JENNIFER	If you don't know, you haven't been.
ALBERT	It's hard to know, with you.
JENNIFER	You don't know me.
BOB	Ladies and —

ALBERT   —You live with someone, you'd think you'd know
              them. You'd think you could trust them.

BOB   Excuse me —

JENNIFER   — That's an insult.

BOB   Excuse me —?

JENNIFER   — Take it back.

ALBERT   I never insult anyone. Bob, do I ever —

BOB   Wait a minute. Is anyone interested in this
              experiment?

              Pause.

ALBERT   Sorry Bob.

              Pause.

JENNIFER   Sorry Bob.

ALBERT   Start again, would you, Bob?

              Pause.

BOB   Ladies and gentlemen: we have gathered to witness—

JENNIFER   — Man.

BOB   I'm including myself, Jennifer. I know I'm
              performing the experiment, but I'm a watcher too.
              Because I've never done it before. So, ladies and
              gentlemen: we have gathered to witness an
              experiment. The embodiment of an Idea. We have
              before us a sheet of tin foil. It's been crumpled and
              then flattened out to simulate the pier-glass or
              polished steel referred to in George Eliot's novel,
              Middlemarch.

              Pause.

We have examined the tin foil. We have noted that its surface is covered with minute lines like the scratches on a polished steel surface and we have agreed that the lines go every which way. They form no pattern. Also we have agreed to think of the lines as events.

JENNIFER   I'm not sure I can agree to that.

ALBERT   You already agreed.

JENNIFER   I'm thinking of changing my mind.

ALBERT   Why?

BOB   Is there something wrong with the analogy Jennifer?

JENNIFER   It's vague.

BOB   Okay.

JENNIFER   It's vague and arbitrary.

ALBERT   She just wants to argue.

BOB   Vague and arbitrary.

ALBERT   We agreed that the lines are like events, things that happen in life.

JENNIFER   When? Where? And who to?

ALBERT   To whom.

Pause.

Well, she's always correcting everybody.

BOB   I think we agreed to think of the lines as events because that's what George Eliot tells us to do, and if we want to see how her analogy works, we have to follow her directions.

JENNIFER   Fine. Just go on with it then.

BOB   We don't have to be so vague though. We could narrow it down to events this year, or today...

JENNIFER   Where?

ALBERT   Wherever you want.

JENNIFER   Thank you, Albert. How about this city?

BOB   Okay. This sheet of tin foil represents — this city. Each line on the foil represents an event that is happening — right now — in this city, to the citizens of this city.

ALBERT   That's neat, Bob.

JENNIFER   Does that include us?

ALBERT   Of course it includes us.

Pause.

BOB   And we've agreed, have we? That the lines are random? They go all over the place? There's no pattern to them?

Pause.

JENNIFER   Yes.

ALBERT   Agreed.

BOB   Then I will light a candle.

Pause. BOB lights a candle.

We have agreed, too, that the candle is to represent ourselves?

ALBERT   One self. One candle can only represent one self. Just thought I'd say that before Jennifer did.

JENNIFER   I wish I could think of my self even as steady as a candle flame.

BOB   One self. The egoism, as George Eliot says, of any
                 person.

                    Pause.

                    BOB places the candle on the foil sheet.
                    JENNIFER and ALBERT come closer to look.

                    Long pause.

ALBERT   I can't say I notice anything, Bob.

BOB   No. But wait — Yes, it is like she says. Look closer.
                 Within the candle's light, the lines do seem to
                 arrange themselves in circles.

ALBERT   I guess so.

JENNIFER   Blow it out and light it again.

                    Pause.

                 Yes, it's true, if you look closely.

BOB   It's an illusion of course. By illuminating some of
                 the lines and excluding others, the candle creates
                 the illusion of a pattern of circles, radiating outward
                 from its centre.

                    Pause.

                 Just as the ego produces the flattering illusion of its
                 self at the centre of events.

ALBERT   Right here, right now, in this city....

JENNIFER   In this room....

ALBERT   Each one of us....

BOB   That's right.

And. It's not enough to realize that you think of yourself as the centre of events that in reality don't centre around you. You have to remember that everyone else thinks of themselves the same way.

BOB lights three other candles while he talks and places them in a row on the foil.

ALBERT   Now there's a row of circles. That's neat, Bob.

JENNIFER   What's it prove?

BOB   It doesn't prove anything. It's just a demonstration of a way of thinking.

JENNIFER   What's it supposed to prove? What's it supposed to prove, Bob?

BOB   I just wanted us to think about it, Jennifer.

JENNIFER   Us.

BOB   All of us.

JENNIFER   You hear that, Marie? I don't think your mother gets it, Bob.

                You get it do you, Albert?

ALBERT   Bob's just trying to help.

JENNIFER   Our theory of goodness, is it?

BOB   Wait. Look.

BOB moves the candles very close together

They gather the circles together, almost like one light.

So maybe it's possible to share a perspective? To create a circle other people would want to share?

***

Sitting on Paradise
by Eugene Strickland

*To ensure their inclusion into a new-age condo development,
DOTTIE's husband ROY has started selling off some of her
possessions, through a publication called the Bargain Finder.
Here a young couple (an unemployed tree-hugger and a night
clerk at a 7-11) arrive to look at her prize possession, the brown
room couch. Also present in the scene is ROY's mentor, WOLF.*

DOTTIE

I've made some coffee. And I have some Nanaimo bars ... I must
admit I picked them up at the bakery ... I just don't seem to have the
time to bake anymore. Committee work, you know ... I thought it
would give us a chance to get to know one another. I mean, what are
we but perfect strangers, thrown together by an act of fate, about to
engage in buying ... and selling ... at least considering ... something as
essential to all of our lives, as a couch? I believe one of the problems
in the world today — other than the situation in Quebec — is that we
have a tendency to trivialize these very significant events of our lives.
We ignore. We carry on. We keep our appointments. And yet, our
lives are really nothing but an accumulation of such events — and our
lives pass so quickly ... You're young. You don't know this yet. But
there will come a day when something that may seem quite
insignificant to you now will bring you great pleasure, great
satisfaction. A batch of Yorkshire pudding that turns out "just so!" Or
a certain outfit you agonize about wearing, that looks just so smart,
and is just so suitable to the occasion. Or, indeed, buying a couch.
This couch? Well, we'll see. Certainly you're here. We're here. The
couch is here. Anything seems possible, doesn't it? And isn't that
what Keats meant, when he said,

Heard melodies are sweet, but those unheard
Are sweeter; therefore, ye soft pipes, play on ....

If you buy the couch, just imagine what a beacon it will be on an
otherwise bleak horizon ... how it may inspire you, and challenge you

to rise above your current situation and make something of your lives
... And if you don't buy the couch? What then? If you simply shrug
your shoulders, frown, and walk away from it? What then? Will there
come a day, ten tears from now, twenty years from now, when you'll
suddenly be so overwhelmed with a profound sense of regret that
you'll bury your head in your hands and sob, "If only ... if only we'd
bought that couch!"

The couch has always meant a great deal to us ... Well, to me. And it
still does, in many ways ... Even though it's not fashionable to admit
this, the couch, and many of the other things you see in this house,
indeed, the house itself, have all contributed to our sense of who we
are ... what we are ... but especially the couch, this couch... It is
virtually throbbing with profound significance. I guess it came into our
lives at a time when we needed something, somehow ... something
more than what we had. I don't know how to explain it, but
occasionally we find ourselves having trouble ... difficulty some days,
just getting out of bed in the morning can be a monumental task ...
The couch came along when our lives were quite empty ... lacking
purpose ...direction ... I don't like to suggest it, but I believe this
emptiness may have come as a result of our inability to have children.
We had no children to fill the void that existed in our lives. And
maybe we would have. Maybe we would have tried harder. Maybe we
would have gone so far as to adopt. And yet, along came the couch,
and it filled that void, to a certain extent... And it still does, more than
I can say. As much as anything can fill the void. We may try to fill it
up with great deeds or even questionable spiritual pursuits. For me,
the couch was all I ever needed to keep myself from tumbling
headlong into the yawning abyss (*slight pause*)

Many a time, I've gone up to the brown room ... alone and sat on the
couch ... and felt its sturdy structure supporting my weight, felt the
cushions beneath my thighs, felt the fabric beneath my fingertips all
so comforting ... so reassuring ... and so it's ... it's so very hard to think
of parting with it ... so very hard ... to try to picture my life without it
knowing it's gone somewhere else ... to a different home with new
people — strangers ... sitting on it ... watching TV ... napping —
whatever it is you plan to do on the couch ... it's just so very difficult
to come to grips with it all ... and so I'd feel better, and I hope you
would too, if we could take some time, to get to know one another ...
and have some coffee ... and Nanaimo bars ...

***

MAGPIE

by Kit Brennan

Bernice is a small-town prairie wife with a large fantasy life revolving around the new dance instructor. The play takes place on the day she is to go home from convalescence after a breakdown. The dancer is himself and also, at times, a personification of a magpie, a bird whose flight and ability to be free haunts Bernice. One actor plays the three roles of Doctor, Dave (Bernice's husband), and the Evangelist.

> *The Dancer, curled up on the floor.*
>
> *BERNICE enters, lumpy; she is carrying articles to be packed. She sees the Dancer, stops, ignores him, goes around him. Looks back. Turns away. Looks back.*
>
> *DAVE appears, sitting outside BERNICE's room, cap in hands. BERNICE inches towards the Dancer, trying to coax it. DAVE clears his throat.*
>
> *BERNICE moves away from the Dancer, turns her back to it, her eyes dead, her hands busy.*
>
> *The Dancer begins to move. He rises, arms upraised, on one leg. He spreads his wings, yearning upwards.*
>
> *BERNICE does not look toward the Dancer.*

BERNICE (*whispered, prayed; from hopelessness rising to excitement, through the following:*) And then I said to him I said "I never meant for you to think that. I'd do anything to make you happy I swear to God, and how could you possibly want to break my heart like

this when you know how much I love you." That's
what I said. And he, he cried with joy to hear those
words from my mouth, pouring out of my mouth, it
was beautiful. Truly beautiful. And we collapsed
backwards onto his couch, and he took me then and
there, and the door was closed, and no one saw, but
I saw, I was there. And the Lord God saw that it was
good. It was so good!

> *She sees the audience. The Dancer arrests in
> mid-flight.*

I'm just kidding.

> *The Dancer curls into the floor.*

What? I'm just telling a tale! Don't get me wrong,
OK, it's just a tale told by an idiot, signifying
nothing, right? I bin to school; went back, did night
classes, English lit and that. I know that stuff, eh?

I'm just kidding around.

> *She laughs loudly, stops short; the DOCTOR
> appears, looks at his watch, looks in at her. She's
> aware of him, but does not look at him.*

DOCTOR   Bernice?

BERNICE   What?

DOCTOR   How are you doing in there?

BERNICE   Good.

DOCTOR   Fine. No rush. Let me know if I can help.

BERNICE   Oh I will.

DOCTOR   Another five minutes?

BERNICE   'Bout that.

DOCTOR   ...Right. I'll come for you.

He exits.

BERNICE (*to audience*) What are you looking at? Tell you something I just figured out. So help me God I never knew this before. Listen, maybe this'll help you, you know, you can avoid the heartache I bin through. Listen.

If you have life and energy in you, they want it. They want it so much they'll do anything to rip it out of you. They will. There. You can have that for nothing. Tell that to your kids some dark stormy night, and don't let them tell you you never gave them nothing.

DAVE coughs, fiddles with his cap. She's aware of this sound.

BERNICE (*to audience*) Bet you thought you'd landed in some sort of loony bin, eh? Here's this woman, talking to herself. Chatting away, just chatting and telling tales. But don't you believe it.

It's like I tell my kids, all five of them bright and shiny as new pins — I tell them, you go to school and read books and do what they tell you and you'll go far. You will. Long as you do what they say.

The Dancer begins to rise, as DAVE becomes EVANGELIST.

My life and that's given me this gift, oh yes. I'm here before you, the multitudes. On the air. On the air we reach the people, on the air is freedom. And the time is running out! I found that out for sure and ever, I found that out you know. Well, you can see! And so I'm here to tell you, you in the studio and you in your living rooms there, I'm here to tell you the time is now, the time is writ and burnished in gold! And the face of the world is gonna be changed! You gotta make a change!

> *The EVANGELIST appears, in her mind. The Dancer becomes immobile, out of the range of the EVANGELIST's gaze.*

EVANGELIST   Oh no, Bernice, no no.

> *BERNICE freezes.*

BERNICE   ...What was I saying? (*carefully*) I've been resting, eh? I been taking on too much, I always do that. And I've got to be careful. If I don't, I'm gonna die. I will.

> *The EVANGELIST fades away. She waits, then:*

See this dress? He gave it to me. 'Cause he thinks I'm so beautiful, he got it for me and no one else in the whole world has a dress like this. No one. It's one of a kind, like me. That's what he says, I'm not making it up, he tells me embarrassing stuff like that and I say Shh! what are people going to think, you talking to me like that and you my teacher. They don't like that, they don't like that kind of life and love going on right under their noses you know. They'll say anything to stop it. 'Cause they're afraid. They're afraid of it.

> *The Dancer begins, carefully, to strut.*

And I've got to be careful, so careful. Cause I'm delicate. That's what he tells me, he says you're so delicate Bernice, you're just like a little china figurine. If I was to put you on one of those things that go round, like on a music box you know with the snow and the glass bubble and that, why then I'd put you way up high where no one could come along and knock you off by accident, no one could whoops with their elbow and make you fall and spill your waters all over the floor, and break you into little pieces no way. No more. And God said Let the waters under the heaven be gathered into one place, and let the dry land appear, and it was so. And it was me. I appeared. And he saw that it was good. (*covering her mouth*) Oh shit. There I go, I'm doing

it again. Those words they keep coming out of my
mouth. Toads. Bunch of toads. Falling out. (*looking
around to be sure she's not being watched*) But I'm
just a silly, that's what my ma used to say, you're
just a big silly Bernice, what are you going on about
now? She'd be so exasperated with me, and I'd
laugh!

She follows the Dancer with her eyes.

You live in your head, Bernice. That's what she'd
say. You just get down to business girl, that'll stand
you in good stead. Steady. Steady on. Steadfast and
that. The steadfast tin soldier, standing on his one
leg, looking at his love. The china ballerina with a
missing leg, just like his. But it isn't missing, see,
that's the thing — it's just hid, up under her skirt.
He just can't see it. So she isn't like him. He's all
alone. Falls into the fire, nobody notices him;
melted and missing parts, thrown out with the ash,
shit on by dogs — (oop, pardon my French) — he
sails off down this sewer pipe, longing for his
ballerina, longing for his one true love. But she's
whole and he's not, and he doesn't even know. Into
the dark and the stench, out of the light of the
world, not one word of blame, not one shout of "—
!" (*inarticulated rage chokes her*)

My kids don't like that one. And I don't blame them.
There's no happy ending. (*picking up and fondling
clothes*)

When I was a girl, I'd go tramping off round the
farm, we had a big farm, it's out near Stony Bend in
Saskatchewan and my dad he raised cattle mostly,
couple pigs. He kept us at it. I'd take a book — I
love to read, I've always loved it, even in high
school when you're not supposed to be interested in
books, you know, but in boys? — I'd take a book, a
romance like or something with a lot of colour. This
book'd be under my arm, and I'd take off in the
spring in my rubber boots, and go walking. I'd be out
for hours; rip off a piece from the wolf willows,
pretend I was in a movie, you know, I'm smoking

this twig all elegant, like Lauren Bacall or Ingrid Bergman in one of those old black and white films ... I wanted a trench coat so bad and my dad said don't be stupid how you going to milk the cows in one of those things. Anyway, there I'd be, each part of the picture I'm in unreeling before me, around me, in me, scene by scene; a captured maiden, a foreign spy, dark deeds and that. I can see them all. I'd park myself under a tree and I'd read and read, and I'd get so, oh, I'd get so into that book, I get so restless and I get so wet I ... anyway, they're calling for me, and I wouldn't hear them. Or maybe I'd be walking back home, I'm walking and they call for me and I look at them and think, who are they talking to? I'd never recognize them. And they'd get so mad! My ma'd shake her head. And my dad'd shake me. But I've always needed that, eh?

> *The DOCTOR enters BERNICE's room.*

DOCTOR   Bernice.

> *The Dancer slips behind, then shadows the DOCTOR.*

BERNICE   Ooops. I'm almost done! I just — some things got put away wrong, that's all. I'm just fixing them.

DOCTOR   Take your time.

BERNICE   I will. I've been resting, so I'm not used to rushing, eh?

DOCTOR   I wanted to make sure you have everything you need.

BERNICE   I do. It's all here.

DOCTOR   Good.

> *He glances at his watch.*

BERNICE   Um .... Doctor?

DOCTOR   Mm?

BERNICE   ...Nothing.

           *Turning, the DOCTOR is frozen in time; the
           Dancer attempts to fly away, but is rooted to the
           ground.*

           (*caressing the Dancer's body*) There's this place I
           know, this place in the park, under the statue; the
           wind doesn't get in there, nor the sun, just the
           darkness, and it's damp and warm, I lie back and I
           feel you, I feel your hands running down my body, I
           feel your need of me and it frightens me because
           I'm too small for you you'll hurt me you'll bruise me
           you'll break my bones and crush me under you, I'm
           delicate and fragile and I'm wet I'm so wet under
           you where it's warm and damp and dark. And I'm —
           uh!

           *She feels inside her clothing, excited, ashamed,
           wet. The Dancer, released, dances away from
           her. Time resumes.*

           ... I've been resting.

DOCTOR   That's good Bernice. Very good.

           *The DOCTOR exits, the Dancer slips out behind
           him and is gone. She yanks all of the packed
           clothing out and begins again, folding, sorting,
           aware of the Dancer's desertion.*

BERNICE   They've got their eyes on me. All of them do, and I
           know why. They can't stand it when one of us gets
           out, gets away from them, escapes!

           They say I live in my head. Well so? So do other
           creative people, so I don't see how that can be bad.
           Inside, I'm an artist, I'm creating all the time, all
           the time. They won't let me watch the soaps, and I
           love those shows, eh? And what's more so does half
           the entire population of the North American
           continent, and half that audience is men sneaking in

to get a daily dose of the lives of their favourites,
right, to know what's going to happen next, to know
what's going to happen!

I miss those shows. They don't want me watching so
much TV.

But what else am I going to do, eh? Got any ideas?
I tell you, without TV most women would go stark
raving mad. I got ideas, I got ideas flying around my
head all the time, but ideas mean money, you got to
have money, your own money, to make ideas come
true. And don't lie to me and tell me that's a load of
shit, because every idea I've ever had it's been shot
down by someone saying to me: you got your
registration fee? you got your membership fee? you
got your student card? you got your Tupperware you
got your wedding band you got your kids?! And if
you think that all doesn't cost big money then
you're nuts. You want to have ideas, you better be
ready to pay for them!

Hey. You didn't come here for this kind of talk and
who the hell am I right. I'm sorry. (*nodding toward
the DOCTOR*) He's probably going to give me hell
anyway. Stick around, you can watch that, there's
something you can get your teeth into. Conflict,
pure and simple. Sure, I know, I'm not stupid. The
six o'clock news, the police car down the street, the
blood on the highway and we slow past gawking. It's
what we live for.

Waiting for something to happen.

He hates it when I get loud, when I get mad and
that. They all do. They don't want to go there with
me. But things just swell up, get red and sore, and
how you gonna let them burst — you take away the
soaps, you take away the romance and that —
where's it gonna go? Eh? That's what they can't tell
me, all their fancy words — that's the little hole in
the logic the water slips through, the hole in the
sock the big toe wiggles out of. Oh yes, there's a
hole. Bigger all the time. And it's in me. In ME! So!

(*small*) ... Come back ...

Hey! I love ideas, eh? I love the way they pop, little explosions, like microwave popcorn, bursting around inside. All contained in your head. Nobody can see them if you don't want them to. They're just *there.* They're sustaining, you know. Nurturing. Nobody can take them away.

She stops what she's doing.

I know what you're thinking. I can see it, I can feel it. How come this woman's using these big words — sustaining, nurturing — she's from Saskatchewan. Oh, I see it. Pretty good, eh? Seeing inside your heads. Well you know what? Bullshit. Bull shit! I bin around, my eyes are open. Who the hell do you think you are? Just who the hell!

The DOCTOR appears.

DOCTOR   Bernice.

BERNICE   What?

DOCTOR   How are you doing? Hm?

BERNICE   I'm doing good.

DOCTOR   Your husband is here. You remember?

BERNICE looks hunted.

BERNICE   Who?

DOCTOR   Dave. He's come to take you home. You're almost ready?

BERNICE   Almost. Soon.

DOCTOR   I know you're feeling uncertain about this, Bernice. But you remember what we talked about?

BERNICE   When.

DOCTOR   This morning. Remember this morning we decided
                — one step at a time. One step, leads to the next, to
                the next. And so we build up confidence.

BERNICE   ... I don't know.

DOCTOR   One task completed. And what was that? You
                remember?

BERNICE   Sure I do.

DOCTOR   ... Yes?

BERNICE   Get up in the morning.

DOCTOR   And?

BERNICE   ... I don't know.

DOCTOR   Make sure your kids get a good breakfast. Before
                they leave for school. Remember?

                She nods.

                And so you're on your way. Each day. A step at a
                time. Now. Can I help you with anything?

BERNICE   No! I mean, I'm fine. For now.

DOCTOR   He's been very patient, Dave. Very understanding.

BERNICE   OK, but I'm just — wait!

DOCTOR   ... With you?

BERNICE   No, just — outside. Just outside.

                He turns, becomes DAVE.

                I know, you know.
                But what else am I gonna do? Eh? How else am I
                gonna ...

(*meaning DAVE*) I see him there. Bin there all the
time, waiting. You see him too, don't you.
I'm not ready for that. Not ready.

***

Plastic Bride

by Shawna Dempsey and Lorri Millan

*Tne Plastic Bride enters through the audience wearing a
bridal gown and veil made entirely of clear plastic, which
contains and reveals her naked body.*

Have you ever had one of those dreams? Where nothing seems to fit
right. You can't find what you're looking for, and the outfit you have
on is, OH, simply inappropriate for the occasion.

You have gone shopping with a friend, your sister or even your own
mother, and been told, "It's perfect. It's you. It's a knockout," only to
find out later that it's a funeral, not a wedding. It's July, not
December. You're a nurse, not an aviator. And the ensemble they
helped you pick out is so wrong, it doesn't even find its way into
Glamour's do's and don'ts. The ensemble they helped you pick out is
so wrong, it should be against the law. There should be laws
protecting against such wrongness, Surgeon General's warnings, and
boycotts. No, the ensemble they helped you pick out is so wrong, that
what they are in fact doing is committing murder 1 or manslaughter
at the very least. But it doesn't matter to you, because by this time
you are stone-cold dead. And this is not a flukish thing like
spontaneous combustion or shark attack. This happens every day.
Violent acts waged by kith, kin, and sales clerks, perhaps without
knowing it, but who cares. The damage is done. And now you are in
purgatory wearing your sin, having broken fashion commandments
left and right. You are in purgatory, and even here the outfit is
WRONG, WRONG, WRONG, except no one here has anything
better to do than laugh at you, to your face this time. And maybe it
shouldn't matter, because you're dead, but it still hurts.

Except, why did you take their advice in the first place? Masochism,
psychosis, a death wish? And even if they hadn't been there, what
would your decision have been? Isn't it possible that you could have
killed yourself just as handily, you, known for your suicidal nature,

by your many style and dress *faux pas* of the past? And haven't you been heard to remark that you would like to end it all, the monthly buying of magazines, the endless wardrobe updates, ever-changing make-up tips and exercise regimes? Isn't it more likely that you are looking for an easy way out? That this fashion self-immolation is merely symptomatic of your ambivalence towards being a woman? This fashion death is merely indicative of your wish for a penis? This unimaginable *grand erreur* reflects jealousy, jealousy of men, just because they can wear the same outfit, day after day, without turning heads. Perhaps you are more than just dead. Perhaps you are sick. Perhaps you are an unnatural woman, who can't seem to remember all of those rules. An unnatural woman, who can't seem to keep those details straight.

(*chewing hand, eyes closed*) There was something I was meaning to say. Something I meant to mean but the meaning's gotten lost and I can't seem to find it anywhere. It, having gotten lost, somewhere.

***

Brave Hearts

by Harry Rintoul

*After a fight at a party, Rafe has waited for the right moment
to leave. Now that he can leave, he discovers that more than
the fight was a deception.*

G.W.   Well things seem to have returned to normal.
              Whatever that is.

RAFE   What?

G.W.   Inside. Things seem to have calmed down. They're
              downstairs playing video games. You could leave
              now, I don't think there'd be a problem.

RAFE   Oh. You know you were asking earlier why I came
              here tonight. I'll tell you if you're still interested.

G.W.   I thought you wanted to go.

RAFE   Yeah I did.

G.W.   You seemed in a big hurry before.

RAFE   That was before.

G.W.   Do whatever you want to.

RAFE   You were asking why I came here tonight, well it
              might sound stupid but, I thought ... I thought I might
              meet someone.

G.W.   That doesn't sound stupid.

RAFE   Bet it's a night Danny won't soon forget.

G.W.	Lighten up. We've been through this.
RAFE	You're right. I did meet someone. I don't even know your name.
G.W.	You can call me G.W.
RAFE	G.W., eh? G.W., I'm Rafe. But you already know that. Thanks.
G.W.	For what?
RAFE	For listening to me.
G.W.	That's me, always in the right place at the right time ...
RAFE	You said I should have more fag friends. So how about it? Friends?
G.W.	Just because I talked to you.
RAFE	And listened. I mean it's not easy for me to talk, but it was easier, it's easy to be honest when you believe that someone really cares and it isn't a game, that they're listening and just not lying to you.
G.W.	I guess it is.
RAFE	Yeah.
G.W.	So I'll be honest with you, you like honesty so much. I lied.
RAFE	What?
G.W.	I lied to you.
RAFE	You're kidding, right?
G.W.	I'm very serious.
RAFE	I don't believe you.

G.W.	Believe me. I thought you wanted to get out of here.
RAFE	I did.
G.W.	Then why didn't you?
RAFE	Everyone was pissed off at me 'cause I punched Danny, he landed on the coffee table ...
G.W.	Danny's fine.
RAFE	What?
G.W.	He's fine. Not a scratch on him.
RAFE	He landed on the coffee table. You said there was blood and glass everywhere.
G.W.	No blood, lotsa glass.
RAFE	You said...
G.W.	After you hit Danny and took off out here, Danny turned to go after you, someone grabbed his arm, he spun around and knocked a twenty-four out of Kenny's arms. It landed on the coffee table.
RAFE	So Danny's not cut up? Kenny doesn't want to beat the crap out of me?
G.W.	He was more worried about the beer than he was about Danny.
RAFE	You said, you told me they were gonna beat the crap out of me, they were inside waiting for me...
G.W.	I told you, I lied.
RAFE	Then they weren't waiting for me?
G.W.	No. Actually Kenny passed out, and they moved the party to the rec room.
RAFE	Then you lied about everything.

G.W.	Yes.
RAFE	Why?
G.W.	You can go.
RAFE	Fuck you. I wanna know what the fuck is going on. Why did you lie?
G.W.	Like I said I wanted to see how you've been, how you were.
RAFE.	Do I believe that?
G.W.	Believe whatever you want to believe.
RAFE	You've lost me.
G.W.	Wouldn't be the first time. Drink your beer. Oh that's right you don't drink. Anymore. You don't have to stay here.
RAFE	What the fuck is going on?
G.W.	You still here?
RAFE	What the fuck is going on here?
G.W.	I told you.
RAFE	I wanna know why you lied.
G.W.	It just happened.
RAFE	It just happened?
G.W.	If it makes you feel any better I didn't mean to.
RAFE	You said you wanted to see how I've been.
G.W.	Grammatical error. I used the wrong tense, excuse me.
RAFE	And what's this, 'You don't drink. *Anymore.*'

G.W. Look, I've told you, you don't have to stay here, you can go.

RAFE I'm not going anywhere until you tell me why you did this.

G.W. And if I don't tell you what are you gonna do, punch me out?

RAFE I believed you because you listened, you make me feel better, then you tell me this. You think it was easy for me to tell you what I did?

G.W. No I don't. But you did tell me.

RAFE Because you kept me here, and I wanna know why.

G.W. (*overlapping*) I told you.

RAFE (*overlapping*) I thought we could be friends.

G.W. (*overlapping*) You don't have to stay here you can go.

RAFE (*overlapping*) Then you tell me you lied to me.

G.W. (*overlapping*) Forget it Rafe, just forget it.

RAFE (*overlapping*) I don't wanna forget it, I wanna know why.

G.W. (*over*lapping) It just happened.

RAFE (*overlapping*) Is this your kick?

G.W. (*overlapping*) Why don't you just leave?

RAFE (*overlapping*) Is this your thing, is it?

G.W. (*overlapping*) Rafe, fuck off, okay?

RAFE (*overlapping*) You get off on this, don't you?

G.W. (*overlapping*) Rafe—-

RAFE	(*overlapping*) I thought you were different.
G.W.	(*overlapping*) Rafe—
RAFE	(*overlapping*) You're no different than anyone else.
G.W.	Raphael.

(*beat*)

RAFE	How do you know my name?

G.W. does not respond.

RAFE	I don't tell anyone that. How do you know that?
G.W.	You don't remember me do you?

RAFE does not respond.

Ask a stupid question.

RAFE	We've met?
G.W.	We've met.
RAFE	I don't remember.
G.W.	That's obvious.
RAFE	When?
G.W.	It was a Saturday night, the August long weekend. I was nineteen. I'll be twenty-six in October, six years ago.
RAFE	Tonight.
G.W.	Really?
RAFE	It's the August long weekend.
G.W.	I never realized.

RAFE	You were nineteen, I was twenty-five.
G.W.	You were driving a Chevy half-ton.
RAFE	I always drive a Chevy.
G.W.	License plate CSW 265.
RAFE	An '82 Silverado. (*pause*) I was drinking then.
G.W.	I know.
RAFE	It's not that I don't believe you.
G.W.	If you'd left when I told you to...
RAFE	But I didn't. I swear to you, G.W., I don't remember you. If you want the truth I don't remember a whole lot.
G.W.	(*overlapping*) That's understandable.
RAFE	I been dry two years now and I still run into people who seem to know me but I ... I don't have a clue who they are, or how we met, or why. Sometimes something just pops into my head, a name, a song, something or someone looks familiar, and I don't know why. I don't remember meeting you. There's a year and a half, two years of my life I can't remember. (*pause*) So how did we meet?
G.W.	Rafe, we don't have to go through this.
RAFE	I do.
G.W.	I was sitting on the grass on Spadina past the park, near the Broadway Bridge, there was this '52 T-Bird. I was looking at the car and the next thing I know there you were. We started talking.
RAFE	And then?

G.W.   You asked me what I was doing. I told you I'd just
            hit town, told you about the old man and you said,
            'Let's go for coffee.'

RAFE   And things went the way they usually do.

G.W.   No. Not at all.

RAFE   Oh?

G.W.   We went for coffee and we talked. Sat in a Country
            Style Donuts talking 'til about four in the morning,
            went for a drive, drove all over town, went back to
            the Country Style, had a bite to eat, talked, then we
            drove around and talked some more.

RAFE   What the hell did we have to talk about?

G.W.   Everything. Books, music, politics, you name it.
            Sports, crops, weather, being fags, everything. We
            just talked, and then about seven in the morning you
            offered me the use of your couch.

RAFE   I didn't ask you to...

G.W.   No. You said sex wasn't everything. That, for some
            reason, impressed the hell out of me.

RAFE   Did we ever—

G.W.   That's not important.

RAFE   I'd like to know.

G.W.   We did, and if you need to know, it was great.

RAFE   I didn't need to know that. Then what?

G.W.   I hung around for a couple of days. You said I could
            stay if I wanted but I wanted to see some friends
            who were living in town. You said I was welcome
            any time. I came by a couple of times after that, but
            you were never home.

RAFE   I was real busy, work was nuts. I wasn't home much.

G.W.   So I stayed with Cindy, my only girlfriend. Found a
             job. I stopped by from time to time but you weren't
             home, and then I went by once and you'd moved.

RAFE   I was working out of Regina for a while, then
             Calgary, I was moving around a lot.

G.W.   I didn't know how to get in touch with you.

RAFE   Why did you want to?

G.W.   You were fun to be with. You could talk a blue
             streak but you listened. I was bust-up about the old
             man kicking me out and you listened. You were a
             friend when I didn't have any friends.

RAFE   It was the booze.

G.W.   It was who you were.

RAFE   I was different then.

G.W.   You're the same person, you just don't have that
             spark you used to have.

RAFE   It was the booze. I was ... I am an alcoholic. I was
             uninhibited when I was loaded, and I was rather
             uninhibited for years.

G.W.   So what happened?

RAFE   I wish I could tell you what one thing it was, if it
             was just one thing. I woke up one morning and it
             wasn't worth it any more. I didn't know where the
             hell I was, who the person next to me was or how I
             got there. I got tired, tired of the one-night stands.
             Whatever thrill there once was in riding all night,
             hoping, searching, just vanished. I was drinking too
             much. I'd go to bed drunk, wake up half-drunk, be
             drunk by lunch. I almost killed a guy driving home
             one night. My parents died. Two years ago. A drunk.
             Crossed over the centre line. Hit 'em head on. And

	all this time ... I don't know what happened, I just know it did.
G.W.	I'm sorry about your folks.
RAFE	Thanks. So ... what was tonight all about then?
G.W.	I wanted to see you and talk to you.
RAFE	I don't recognize you.
G.W.	I knew it was you the minute I saw you.

***

Maggie's Last Dance

by Marty Chan

A high school gym decorated for a dance. A glowing disco ball shoots out pinpoints of light. Hard metals chairs line both sides of the gym — the boys' side and the girls' side.

> *"Stayin' Alive" by The Bee Gees is playing. JIM, at 16, struts across the stage.*

JIM
Francis Langley High School. First dance of the year. And Jim Bauer's got "Saturday Night Fever". I'm hot. Even the grade eleven babes are checking me out. Well, they've got a lot to look at. Shirt. 100 percent velour. V-necked. Opened just enough to reveal my two neatly groomed chest hairs. Pants: bell bottoms. Shoes. Standard two-inch platforms. Jacked up an inch, thanks to shims from shop class. Clothes by Woolco. Attitude by Foreigner. "Cold as Ice". Keep playing it cool. only nerds dance this early.

> *DERRICK and HELEN come out and dance. They are 16.*

Later in the dance, Derrick Sackett and Helen Barbour slow dance to the Commodores, "Three Times a Lady". Derrick's hand slides down to Helen's butt. She slides it up. His other hand drops. Helen shoves it back. He tries again and again and again. It's like watching a perpetual drinking bird.

> *ELLA and CHRISTINE (16) enter.*

They distract me so much that I almost miss her arrival. The hottest girl in grade 10. Ella Givens. She's everything Joanie Cunningham is and more. Much more. If only I could be her Chachi. I've had this thing for her since she said she'd help me study Social. She scans the gym. I see her head flick in my general direction. Cool, she wants me. Got to make my move soon. Next song, I promise. It comes up faster than I expect. Da Do Ron Ron. She jumps up with her friends and they all go Cassidy Crazy. I think I'll wait.

Next song comes up. Leo Sayer's "You Make Me Feel Like Dancing". A cool song. A danceable song. A song where couples are made. The other guys sense this. They launch from the safety of the bleachers. They want to glide like Tony Manero, but they shuffle like Tim Conway. Still, they move closer to the promised land. If I wait, someone else might ask her. I have to make my move now.

I join the race everyone wants to win but no one wants to lead. I make it past the chaperone. Past groping couples. Past the volleyball line. Mid point. No turning back. I smell the sweet aroma of Pert wafting from her Farrah Fawcett hair.

Breath gets short. Legs shaky. My zits on hi beam. Velour shirt suddenly feels very heavy. She looks at me. I make a right angle turn and head to the punchbowl. I slug back two glasses of orange punch. Liquid courage. Okay, I'm going to do it now. I spin around to see ... her empty chair. I scan the girl's side of the gym. No one's there except Christine McCoy. She flashes me a smile. The disco light bounces off her braces and blinds me. I look to the dancing couples.

ELLA dances with STEPHEN.

Oh man, she's dancing with Stephen Nesbitt. Mr. Hockey, Basketball, Volleyball, Highest marks in Grade 10, Drives his Own Car. What's he got that I don't? He tells her a joke. She laughs. He leans in. She lets him. She touches his arm. If they slow dance, I'm done for.

"Swayin' to the Music" by Johnny Rivers plays now. STEPHEN clinches ELLA.

Fifty glasses of punch later, the punchbowl is nothing more than a mound of wet sugar. On the floor, old and new couples clinch. And in the middle Stephen clings to her. Francis Langley High School. First dance of the year. I'm alone and my bladder hurts.

He exits.

***

Armagideon

by Sandra Dempsey

*A mysterious, multi-layered and disturbing tale about two
elderly "aunts" Molly and Violet, their 9 year-old ward
Seanasy, and their soldier "nephew" Nathan. All confront
and seek to cope with the grim reality of surviving nuclear
warfare.*

> *NATHAN has risked military reprisal and come
> to the house of MOLLY and VIOLET to warn his
> "aunts" of the new danger of impending warfare
> in the area, and to take custody of SEANASY.*

VIOLET   Nathanial, we were all born into LD-50's[1] — and
once they figured out how big a dose they needed to
kill half of us, the rest were free to go.

We came out alright, didn't we?

MOLLY   (*reminiscing*) I remember like it was yesterday.
There was even a cute little guinea pig — they
force-fed her a lethal dose of heavy water 'til she
died convulsing and vomiting.

NATHAN   But nobody can guarantee you'll both get into the
right fifty per cent!

VIOLET   *Both* of us? What about Seanasy?

NATHAN   He's gotta come with me. Where is he?

---

[1] LD-50 is a test whereby progressively-increasing doses of a
chemical or substance are administered to a group of subjects until
half the group dies — this determines the maximum dose tolerated.

MOLLY   Haven't seen him lately.

VIOLET   If you're so worried about getting caught just visiting, what sort of horrible punishment do you think they've got for *aiding and abetting* a couple of dangerous old fugitives like us? Use your head for once, boy.

We might be *Expendable-Area-Populace*, but we won't be herded off to the badlands again — not like the pair of diseased vermin you think you're responsible for! I'm gonna live out my last days in this house — and no amount of nonsensical military manipulation is gonna change that!

As for Seanasy, your *Happy Cappy Herod* has the entire male species under his command. He's not gonna miss one little nine-year-old. Wear your stripes on your sleeve for once, boy — not your brain!

NATHAN slams his fist into the wall.

Nathan, calm down.

MOLLY   Knuckle-splints won't help anybody!

VIOLET   'Least of all you.

Come on now. Come sit next to me, there's a boy.

She exchanges a look with MOLLY.

Now, supposing, just supposing, we *were* to leave — we couldn't just wander off into the wilderness without protection, now could we? Why don't you tell us all about your favourite subject — what kind of *guns* we should take? Hmmm?

MOLLY   It'll take your mind off things, dear. 'Always does!

VIOLET   What would you suggest for your silly old Aunts?

NATHAN finally gives in and quietly moves to sit on the couch..

NATHAN	(*the more he speaks, the more excited and animated he gets*) Well ... Uh, there's two classifications to consider, okay? One's Defensive and the other's Offensive...
MOLLY	Oh, let's take the friendly kind!
NATHAN	Uh, that's right! Ya want Defensive weapons! Ya want at least two handguns apiece — but not home-builts; they'd probably just blow yer fingers off. A semi-automatic is best — smooth action, minimum 15-round clip — and you'll need t'carry at least two extra clips — I'd suggest a nice Glock with jacketed soft-points[2] — that would do ya just fine. Ya can pick those up easy over at the market.
MOLLY	"Glock!" Is that short for "glockenspiel?"
NATHAN	Uh, no...
VIOLET	(*to NATHAN*) Now, don't you feel better? Look at how much more relaxed you are, telling us what you know best, putting our minds at ease!
MOLLY	(*she holds up the dead bird*) Oh look what I found in the back yard today! Isn't he pretty!? Must've been dead a good week by the look of him!
VIOLET	(*through gritted teeth*) You mean when you were exercising your "Priority Travel Fallout Sojourn in the Countryside", right, dear?
MOLLY	(*catching on*) Oh, um, yes, that's what it was...
	MOLLY begins to prepare the carcass for taxidermy.
VIOLET	That's right, Molly.
	Go on, Nathan. Please continue.

---

[2] Jacketed soft-points are soft or hollow-tipped bullets designed to expand upon impact. Condemned for war use on humans by The Geneva Convention.

MOLLY   (*she reads from the instructions as she works*) "Birds. Place Kleenex in throat...

NATHAN   (*he jumps back in excitedly*) You'll need some *Anti-Pers* [3] mines — say, twenty or so — each one'll give ya one thousand 4-millimetre steel cubes or six hundred 6-millimetre ball bearings exploding at groin-level — an' that's good, 'cause it'll give a severe wound, but it *won't kill* — an' a wounded man'll delay yer enemy much more effectively than a killed man...

MOLLY   "Tuck head under wing. Place bird in newspaper cone for protection..."

VIOLET   Molly, not another magpie — please! You've already got more than you know what to do with...

NATHAN   (*almost dancing with excitement*) Ya could get a couple of *Colt DEA's*[4], for reserve — 9 millimetre, over eleven hundred rounds-per-minute — that'll stand up pretty good against an AK-47 or an Uzi[5] ...

MOLLY   (*she's made an extra newspaper cone and wears it on her head*) "Place bird and cone in plastic bag and freeze."

VIOLET   The freezer's full t' bursting, Molly! Be reasonable now... (*she's cut off*)

NATHAN   (*jumping in, louder*) But what ya have t' have fer yer main protection is a couple of *C-MAG's*[6] — one each — fully automatic, it's small, an' it'll only give ya a hundred continuous rounds, an' the bullets *are* smaller, full-metal jacket[7] — but, see, the

---

[3] Anti-Pers is the military slang for anti-personnel — pronounced anti-*PURSE*.

[4] Small hand-held fully-automatic firearm — pronounced *Colt dee-ee-ay*.

[5] Uzi is an assault rifle — pronounced *oo-zee*.

[6] C-MAG's are fully-automatic rifles — pronounced *see-mags*.

[7] Full-metal jacjet is the description for a solid-point bullet designed to reduce expansion on impact — The Geneva Convention decreed

jacket's a lot *thinner* so the round'll fragment easy
on impact and give ya a more *severe* wound.

'See, when the bullet enters the flesh, it goes in an'
then it *rotates*, an' *then* it *fragments*, 'cause of the
bend-stress on the bullet during rotation! An' that's
what ya want! Ya *want* yer bullet t' penetrate yer
enemy but *not go straight* through, 'cause it could
hit a friendly[8]

> *He's almost orgasmic.*

An' then there's the *AA-1 Fleshette*[9] — that'll
penetrate right through the spaces in the mesh of
body-armour, an' then, when it bends on impact, it
explodes thousands of tiny metal darts! One
*beautiful ballistically induced aperture in the
subcutaneous environment!*

> *There is a violent thunderclap and immediate
> heavy rain.*

***

---

that this type of bullet *must* be used in war on humans — opposite of
soft-point.

[8] Friendly refers to one of your own — opposite of *hostile* or *enemy*.

[9] AAI Fleshette is an armour-piercing, schrapnel-exploding bullet —
pronounced double-ay-one flesh-ette.

The Maltese Bodkin

by David Belke

*This play is a comedy hybrid: a 1930's film noir mystery set in
the London of William Shakespeare. Aside from the lead
detective character, all the suspects and supporting
characters are drawn directly from the works of William
Shakespeare. The mysterious client is Viola from "Twelfth
Night", the hired thug — Iago from "Othello", the local
source of street-level information is Sir John Falstaff, and
lurking behind the scenes playing the role of the villainous
mastermind is Richard, Duke of Gloucester soon to be
"Richard III". This monologue is the opening to the play and
is delivered by the lead character, hard-boiled detective
BIRNAM WOOD.*

> *Scene is darkness to begin, a dim light resolves
> itself on a solitary figure as a lonely saxophone
> wails in the background. The figure is a man,
> dressed in a trenchcoat and fedora. A cigarette
> dangles from his mouth. This is BIRNAM WOOD,
> private investigator. The character serves as
> narrator through his monologues and will always
> come back to the same position and light to
> resume his narrative role. He is trying to light his
> cigarette with a very uncooperative lighter. He
> is unable to get any sort of flame. He becomes
> more and more frustrated.*

WOOD

(*angry, cursing the lighter*) 0, for a muse of fire ... (*he pockets the
lighter*) The world's a lousy place sometimes, and sometimes the
worst thing about it can be the place you find yourself in. Like I
never wanted to find myself in London. Especially not in 1605. Lousy
year. Lousy town. Mud-caked, tumble-down old dive. With the best-

kept lawns in all the world. Wasn't my kind of town. Too foggy. Too snooty. Too ... Jacobean.

But you gotta make do with where you're at and running the P. I. game with Archie Heath was one of the few good things that had happened to me since I got there. Archie was a good egg. Maybe a little too soft-boiled for his own good, but he was the best damn pal I ever had. The street work was my job. Business was good. Maybe too good.

That's how I ended up out of the country when the spit hit the fan. And when I got back, there was a pile of unfinished reports, the office was a mess, and Archie ... my partner Archie Heath was dead.

I hit rock bottom. I was in a hole so deep I could smell the tea brewing in China. I crawled inside a bottle and screwed the cap shut. My luck had run dry. But luck is a lot like life. You gotta go all the way to find it. And luck was about to walk through the door...

***

Speak

by Greg Nelson

The place is Regina, Saskatchewan. The time: the present.
James Gallagher, 30 years old, has come to visit his former
boss, Lloyd Thomas, 50. Two years ago, the two men were
lawyers working together at a Regina law firm. James has
since moved away to Toronto; Lloyd has gone into politics —
he is now a Saskatchewan MLA. They haven't seen each
other for two years.

> *LLOYD's office, at the Legislature, JAMES is at*
> *the door. He has just come in. LLOYD stares at*
> *him for a moment.*

LLOYD	Jamie Gallagher.
JAMES	Hello Lloyd.
LLOYD	(*slight pause*) I didn't know you were in town.
JAMES	Well—
LLOYD	I spoke to your wife. Sarah.
JAMES	Yes.
LLOYD	On the phone. She said you weren't in town.
JAMES	She didn't know I was coming, I just suddenly hopped on a plane...
LLOYD	I see
JAMES	I haven't been back for... Well, for two years. So I thought ... you know...

LLOYD   I see.

                    Pause. LLOYD stares at him.

                    You know, I used to dream about this moment.

JAMES   Do you want me to go?

LLOYD   No—

JAMES   I'd understand, if you'd rather not...

LLOYD   No, no, I'm .... actually, I'm pleased to see you.

JAMES   Really?

LLOYD   Oh yes, I'm delighted.

JAMES   Are you sure?

LLOYD   Sit down.

JAMES   Thank you.

                    LLOYD gazes at JAMES. Pause.

LLOYD   Life is funny. Just the other day, I was thinking about you.

JAMES   Really?

LLOYD   I'd been thinking about Michelle. What she'd been through. Her life, her journey. And I thought to myself, "I wonder. Has Jamie had one too? A journey? What's become of Jamie?"

JAMES   Huh.

LLOYD   I imagined us meeting again. And what I would say to you. And right then, right at that moment, the phone rang ... and it was Sarah.

JAMES   Really.

LLOYD   It was your wife.

JAMES   You're kidding.

LLOYD   I'm not kidding.

JAMES   That's funny.

LLOYD   Isn't that funny? I knew something was happening.
        Something was going on. And you know what I did?
        I closed my eyes, and said a prayer. Just a short
        prayer. Guess what I prayed for.

JAMES   What?

LLOYD   You James. I prayed for you.

JAMES   Huh. Well, thank you.

LLOYD   You're welcome.

        Pause.

JAMES   So, how is Michelle?

LLOYD   Oh, she's doing very well. She's off the Prozac now.

JAMES   She...

LLOYD   You knew she was suicidal.

JAMES   Really.

LLOYD   Oh yes. For two years. Ever since you left, as a
        matter of fact.

JAMES   I, no. I didn't know, I mean, I've *thought* about her,
        you know, I, I, I wondered ... but I didn't...

LLOYD   She's much better now.

JAMES   Good.

LLOYD Much much better. She's doing really well. Really great.

JAMES (*slight pause*) Well. Tell her I say 'Hello'.

LLOYD I can't do that James.

JAMES Why not?

LLOYD I'm not allowed to see her. Or to speak with her.

JAMES You... *Oh*...

LLOYD I lost her. I lost my family. My wife, my daughter. I just... threw them away.

JAMES Gee, I'm... I'm sorry... I didn't know.

Pause.

LLOYD And you. How are you

JAMES I'm good.

LLOYD You got married.

JAMES Yes.

LLOYD Good for you. Sarah Peters.

JAMES That's her.

LLOYD I've just been reading her book.

LLOYD has the book in his desk. He takes it out.

JAMES Really?

LLOYD *Perfect Strangers.* I picked it up last night. After she called.

JAMES What did you think?

LLOYD (*slight pause*) What did I think.

JAMES   Yeah.

                Pause.

LLOYD   Well, frankly, I was prepared to dislike it. I thought to myself "What kind of woman would marry Jamie Gallagher? What kind of book would she write?" But then ... once I picked it up, I couldn't put it down. I thought it was...

                He pauses.

                ...profound and moving. And honest. And just. You know what I thought? I liked *her* — the author, the voice. She has a knowledge, about the world and ... people. She, I felt that she could see inside me. That she somehow knew me. I found myself weeping.

                He looks at JAMES.

                And then I imagined her with you. And what you would do to her. To that ... delicate voice. The damage. And suddenly, I felt cold, I couldn't sleep. I lay in bed, all night ... shivering.

                Pause.

JAMES   Okay. Uh... I understand why you would say that. Given, you know... But, Lloyd, believe me, I would never have come here today if, if... Did Sarah mention that we saw you on TV ?

LLOYD   Yes.

JAMES   When I saw that you had changed... That you'd become a Christian. I knew it would be okay. To come here. Because you're obviously a different person. And this is what I want to tell you...

LLOYD   I am different.

JAMES   Right

LLOYD   I'm completely different.

JAMES   Right, and I could see that. And, and the thing is, Lloyd, the thing is ... I'm different too. Okay? I've changed too. I mean, it's two years later, and, I mean, I'm not a Christian, I didn't go *that* far, but, but I did get married, okay? I got married. To Sarah. And that's a big thing. That changes a man. Completely. The point is: I'm not doing anything to her. Okay? She's done something to me. She's changed me. Because, in your case you, what, you "met Christ" right? (*beat*) Well, I met Sarah. And frankly, I think it's probably very similar.

          Slight pause.

          I'm sorry. Is that offensive?

LLOYD   No.

JAMES   I'm not ... blaspheming, or, or...

LLOYD   Not at all.

JAMES   I mean, I look back on who I was, that guy, that *you* knew, and I think. "Who was that?" You know? "Who was that ... *guy,* that ... awful *guy* ... that *jerk*?"

          He laughs suddenly.

          I mean, God! I was such a jerk!

          More of the laughter. LLOYD says nothing — just sits there, looking at JAMES, and breathing.

          I just. I wanted you to know that. And, uh ... And I wanted to ... apologize. For what I did. It was unforgivable, it ... And I'm sorry.

          Pause.

LLOYD   Can I tell you something?

JAMES   Yes, of course.

LLOYD	I'm frightened.
JAMES	Frightened.
LLOYD	Yes.
JAMES	Of what.
LLOYD	I've been trembling. Ever since you came in.

Slight pause.

Do you remember the last time you saw me? It was in Toronto. It was the middle of the night. I came to your apartment. I'd just flown in, from Regina, and I banged on your door, and started shouting. I was drunk. You threatened to call the police. Because I had a gun, Remember? I was drunk, and raging, and I had a gun, and I told you I was going to shoot you. Kill you.

Slight pause.

Do you remember that?

JAMES	Uh huh.
LLOYD	I could have done it. In that moment. I was capable of killing you. I was in a rage.

He pauses.

It's still inside me, James. Right now, right this second, I can feel it. I am full of ... violence.

***

Poor Superman

by Brad Fraser

*David, a successful gay painter, has recently had a difficult
and ultimately unsuccessful affair with a married man. This
affair was exposed by his friend Kryla, a high profile
newspaper columnist. In this scene from the final movement
of the play, Kryla confronts David about the lies he told her
while embroiled in the affair. David, in turn, tells Kryla about
the suicide of their mutual friend Shannon, an HIV-positive
pre-op transsexual. This scene is the end of a very long and
complicated friendship.*

DAVID enters, seeing KRYLA, who sees him.

KRYLA   I didn't tell her.

DAVID   It doesn't matter.

KRYLA   It matters to me.

DAVID   It had nothing to do with you.

KRYLA   Fags think they're persecuted but they're not. Not the same way women are. Fags're still men. At least they're "men." They don't get lied to. No one tells them they'll be taken care of. No one tells them everything's gonna be all right.

DAVID   What's your point?

KRYLA   Everything's easy for you.

DAVID   You're an alcoholic.

KRYLA   You're a drug addict. And an alcoholic.

DAVID	You're bitter.
KRYLA	You're manipulative.
DAVID	You're more manipulative.
KRYLA	I have to be. It's the only way we're allowed to accomplish anything.
DAVID	Us too.
KRYLA	You said you weren't sleeping with him.
DAVID	It was nonna your business.
KRYLA	Friends don't lie to each other.
DAVID	Of course they do. We all lie to each other. It's what we're taught. It's how we learn to communicate.
KRYLA	You broke up that marriage.
DAVID	It would've been fine if you'd stayed out of it.
KRYLA	A cheating husband isn't fine just because the wife doesn't know.
DAVID	Matt made his own decisions.
KRYLA	You're smarter than he is.
DAVID	That gives you the right to interfere in my life?
KRYLA	What you were doing was wrong.
DAVID	Why? Because they're married?
KRYLA	No, because he said he'd never fuck anyone else.
DAVID	We all say that. And most of us mean it. For varying lengths of time.
KRYLA	It's not a fucking joke.

DAVID   You're a fucking joke.

KRYLA   You lied to me!

DAVID   You're a bitter unhappy frustrated woman!

KRYLA   You're a fag. You can't change that. No matter how
               many straight men you get involved with. You'll
               never be like them.

DAVID   Shut up.

KRYLA   You're just a fucked-up kid still wanting your
               straight cousin or anyone like him to use you.

DAVID   Fuck you!

KRYLA   I'm so sick of your whining and moaning. No one
               understands you. You never get the breaks. All your
               friends are dying ...

DAVID   Don't.

KRYLA   People die of other things too you know. Women die
               of all sorts of things. What about breast cancer?

DAVID   And just how many friends have you lost to breast
               cancer? This year.

KRYLA   Two.

DAVID   Twelve to AIDS. This year. You'll excuse me if I'm
               too busy to do anything but wave at the breast
               cancer float.

KRYLA   You make me sick.

DAVID   Shannon's dead.

KRYLA   What?

DAVID   She's doing it right now. She's doing herself before
               the cancer does.

KRYLA   Oh Jesus.

DAVID   And we're standing here arguing about whose pain
               is the most valid.

KRYLA   David ... I'm sorry... I'm sorry...

               *KRYLA puts her arms around DAVID. He remains
               perfectly rigid, unmoving. After a moment she
               lets go of him.*

KRYLA   You have to let it out.

DAVID   If I start crying now I'll never stop.

KRYLA   Why didn't you tell me when you came in? Why
               didn't you stop me? Jesus, David....

DAVID   You're right what you said about my cousin, about
               straight guys — I don't know if I can change it but I
               want to try. I think I have to let go ...

KRYLA   Of me?

DAVID   Of a lot things.

KRYLA   Of me?

DAVID   Yeah.

               DAVID exits.

                            ***

Atlantis

by Maureen Hunter

*Ben is a Canadian living in self-imposed exile on the Greek
island of Santorini. We don't know why he's there; we only
know that he's retreated into silence, and has begun to carve
scraps of wood he picks up as he wanders the island. We also
know he's fascinated with the ancient civilisation that once
flourished there. In this monologue, very early in Act One,
the romance of the past is juxtaposed with the intense
isolation and pain of the present.*

BEN

There's something about being in exile that makes you feel like
Ulysses. You're always searching for Ithaca

Even when you think you're not.

This morning I went as usual to the dig. As usual they turned me
away. I'm not allowed to work there; why, I couldn't say. Because
I'm not an archeologist? I don't speak Greek?

I show up every morning, anyway. They grin, and shake their heads.
They think I'm a little slow.

They don't know that I'd do anything, any kind of labour, just for the
chance to move among them, in that ancient city, just to watch them

Brushing the dust from pieces of antiquity. From pieces of Atlantis!

After a while I wandered off towards Perissa. Looking for my scraps
of wood. I bent to pick one up, and suddenly

Found myself transported back to Lake Marguerite. I don't mean just
in memory; I mean I actually stood there, on the porch overlooking

the lake. In the distance that familiar ring of hills. It was August, a little after dawn: the sun hovered just above the graveyard. There was a breeze rising from the lake; it set the willows trembling. On the breeze the faint enticing smell of new-mown hay.

It was the smell of hay, I think, that did it. I smelled the hay, and then the scene dissolved. I found myself on Santorini, washed in pain.

I remembered I'm alone. I've lost it all.

***

Play Memory

by Joanna McClelland Glass

*The decline and fall of an alcoholic's family. Cam, a dynamic
and successful salesman on the prairie, loses his lucrative
job, threatens the very survival of Ruth, his wife and Jean, his
daughter, and, finally, evicts them from the house in order to
ensure their survival.*

JEAN   I will not stay here ...

RUTH   (*grabbing JEAN*) Yes, you will! Stay and learn how
                to handle a man like this! God forbid, you might
                marry one someday.

                She pushes JEAN into a chair.

                Sit down! And listen! And get some steel in that
                spine of yours. And it doesn't take mental resources
                to have a good fight; all it takes is sticking power.

                *She whirls on CAM, doing the mental equivalent
                of rolling up her sleeves.*

                You're damned right I relate to work! I'm proud of
                that. I *relate* to a minimum wage.

                *The two of them now prowl around JEAN, who is
                penned in a chair. There is a great deal of humour
                underlying each of their arguments.*

CAM   That's what these prairie farm girls relate to! The
                minimum. That's what they aspire to — the
                minimum. When you have no history, no culture,
                you're thankful when they give you a dollar and a
                quarter an hour for back-breaking, mind-boggling,

monotonous work. And then she comes home and delivers herself of her small, diffuse, minimal thoughts!

RUTH You were offered a job last week, you bastard. (*to JEAN*) Driving the elevator at the Connaught apartments. (*back to CAM*) At a minimum wage, yes, and you sitting here without two cents to rub together, and you turned it down. Explain to me why you can't drive an elevator!

CAM I *can* drive an elevator! I won't drive an elevator!

RUTH You drove a car for thirty years!

CAM A car goes horizontal, Ruth, natural, like the land. Oh, you'd be happy, wouldn't you, having me stand in a claustrophobic cubicle with my hand on a clutch all day — me, with my gift of gab; reduced to ... (*he uses a falsetto*) "Going Up," "Going Down," spending the next twenty years driving *vertical* at a minimum wage! (*to JEAN*) Do you know what your mother did on her eighteenth birthday? She was let off the farm for the first time, and she caught a bus into the city, and she went directly to the ladies room at Eaton's. And she stood there the entire day, watching the toilet flush at Eaton's department store. *Mesmerized* at the miracle of modem plumbing because, you see, she'd peed in a hole in an outdoor biffy all her life. On my eighteenth birthday, I went with my grandfather to my great-grandfather's grave. Major David MacMillan of the Third Dragoon Guards. Major David fought with Wellington, at Waterloo, and saved his life, and was decorated afterward. And the Duke of Wellington *gave* Major David a tract of land in Canada. And *that* is how the MacMillans came to these shores!

RUTH (*to JEAN, but for CAM's benefit*) You're a fool if you're impressed with all that hogwash. It's all dead stuff, a lot of old bones in graveyards. I never heard of it 'til he lost the job, then all of a sudden the MacMillans were bloody nobility! My history I seen with my own eyes! Now listen to this. I was ten and there were six kids younger, and I was drug out of school in second grade. Kept home, to mind all those kids. And one day Mum and Dad were out with the plough, and who comes roaring across the land but Indians! Wild Indians! We seen 'em on the horizon, comin' bareback on horses. If you left two sacks of milled white flour, they didn't burn your house. So I left the flour and I ran all the kids up to the attic, and I bolted the trap door. (*pause*) Now, that is impressive. I *remember* that. Nobody *told* me that. I'm a daughter of pioneers, strongest stock on this prairie, and no man anywheres'll make mincemeat of me! (*CAM and RUTH now revert from JEAN to each other*)

CAM
You're an illiterate, peasant, German-descended country bumpkin!

RUTH
And you're a wordy, Scots-descended, whiskey-sodden son-of-a-bitch!

CAM
I am Canadian aristocracy!

***

Elephant Wake

by Jonathan Christenson & Joey Tremblay

*JEAN-CLAUDE is the last remaining resident of an isolated
francophone hamlet called Ste. Vierge, in Saskatchewan.
Throughout the play Jean-Claude reminisces about the glory
days of Ste. Vierge before its residents were lured away by
the thriving economy of the neighbouring anglophone
community of Welby. The cultural vitality of Ste. Vierge is
embodied for Jean-Claude in the large papier maché
elephant he built with his grandmother when he was a child.
Here, he reveals how the elephant met its end and his vision
for a revitalized Ste. Vierge.*

JEAN-CLAUDE

The first time I'm drunk is with 'tit Loup. Memère was gone to visit
in Regina, and me, I was supposed to keep care of the house. 'Tit
Loup said, "Hey! Let's have a party. We'll tell some guys in Welby
and we'll have a party in the big house." Me, I'm nervous. I don't
want a fucking party. But 'tit Loup say, "Come on Choux gras. Don't
be an old lady. Let's have some fun. It's so boring in Ste. Vierge."

When the bar in Welby closes they all show up. Eight ball. Bobby
Welcher. Minty. That stupid Murray Lloyd. All the gang. All the ones
that never talk to me but when there's a party they all show up with
their case of fucking Molson beer and they act like your best fucking
friend.

Me, you know, I'm so nervous. I drink a lot and I drink fast. I'm
nervous because I don't want these maudit anglais to wreck the
house. I heard there was a fight out side and I don't want that in the
house.

Bobby Welcher, him, he's in the middle of the room stomping his foot so hard. All the windows are shaking. The girls are drunk and they're laughing at him, but he just keeps dancing like a big joke.

'Tit Loup, he tells me, "You're acting so weird, Choux Gras. Don't worry.

Everybody is having a good time. Tomorrow we can clean. Go get another beer."

When I go in the kitchen I see that stupid Murray Lloyd. And he's got eggs from the fridge and he's breaking them on the floor. Everybody is laughing. It's supposed to be a funny fucking joke.

"Don't do that, Murray. It's not so funny."

And I go to pick up the mess. And Murray, he breaks an egg on my head. And everyone is laughing at me. And I try to get up but I slip on some eggs. I want to find 'tit Loup. I want him to make everybody go away from Memère's big house. I don't want this party anymore.

When I find 'tit Loup he's holding some girl. He's got his face pressed against some girl's face ... and his tongue is all ... his tongue is all ... And the room is spinning. And Bobby Welcher is dancing. And the windows are shaking. And I have to run outside. I've got shit in my hair and I'm gonna be sick. And I run down the road. I run and I run like I think I'm going crazy. And when I get to the church I stop, and I look up, and in the window upstairs I see the moon. I see the moon in the window of the Ste. Vierge church. And just before I puke all over the gravel, I yell, "God fuck the Queen!"

That's when I hear a noise. The noise of a car that slam its brakes on the gravel road. And a bang, like it hit something. And I see the lights of a car down by Memère's house. And I hear, "What the fuck did we hit?"

Run. Run back to the house. Run to the circle of guys standing on the gravel road.

I see Eight ball. I see Bobby Welcher. I see that stupid Murray Lloyd.

"Hey J.C., maybe you should put up a sign on the road: Elephant Crossing."

And I see my elephant down on the road. In the light of the car that hit him. On the road like this ... with his side smashed in ... and his head all twist like this ... and his sad stone eyes fall out on the gravel with red Christmas paper showing through ... just like blood.

Me, I'm like ice and I can't move. I'm scared to talk because maybe I might cry.

"Who put that guy on the road?"

"Maybe he walk out all by himself."

"Shut up, Murray!"

It's 'tit Loup. And I see him there holding hands with the girl he kiss in the house. And I see something in his dirty half-breed face. And I start to get hot, so hot. And I know. I remember the scarecrow and I know.

"Maudit fucking Métis!"

And I swing my fist like I never did before and I crack him one in the face. And the girl, she scream when 'tit Loup, him, he fall down on the road holding a hand full of blood. And I yell, swinging at all of them, "Everybody go. Everybody go away or I'll kill you. I'll kill you."

(*angry at himself for letting the audience see him cry*) There's no time to cry. There's no time to act sad. If you act sad you're just being fucking lazy. When my Memère died ten years ago I didn't cry. I didn't cry. I didn't cry. I was too fucking busy. I have to clean the house. I have to change all the sheet in the bed. I have to make *tortière, sucre en crème, pâté de fois.* I work and work. The church, too, I clean. I scrape the bird shit from the bench. I shake the mice out of the tabernacle. I even wash the big curtain behind the altar.

There's no time to cry. There's no time to act sad. *Il faut être fort. Il faut travailler fort. Travail. Travail. Travail.*

A while ago I go back to the place in the long grass and I find my elephant. There's not much left of him. Just a bunch of junk, you know, wood and old paper and grass growing through it. And there I am in the tall grass with the bones of my elephant. And everything is so quiet. And everything doesn't move. And that's when I heard a whisper, so quiet in my ear, almost like a kiss. And it say, "Hey, funny face! You wanna smoke?" And that's when I get my idea. That's when I know what I'm gonna do.

I'm gonna make an elephant. I'm gonna make an elephant so fucking big that when he stand over the gravel road the cars, they can drive right through his legs. I'm gonna make an elephant so fucking big that the people they can see it from Welby. They can see it from St. Joseph. They can see it all the way from Minot fucking North Dakota. And the people, they're gonna come from all over to see this big fucking guy. They're gonna come from all over the world. And Ste. Vierge ... Ste. Vierge is gonna grow and grow.

> *He returns to ripping paper. As he does so he sings.*

"En passant de la rosier..."

***

Roundup

by Barbara Sapergia

It's a blistering hot day, the annual cattle roundup at Paul and Verna Petrescu's ranch in southern Saskatchewan. After years of drought, the ranch is in trouble and so is the marriage. And their daughter Darcy has some worries of her own.

PAUL   Verna, come outside a moment.

VERNA   Right now? We're almost ready for supper.

PAUL   I don't care about supper.

VERNA   Paul, for heaven's sake.

PAUL   Just come, all right?

VERNA   All right!

VERNA comes outside.

What is it?

PAUL   Are you really saying you don't wanna live here any more?

She doesn't answer.

Tell me why, Vern. I mean, you said you don't like my attitude. Well, what about you? You haven't been so easy to live with lately. Giving me the cold shoulder. Trying to run Darcy's life.

VERNA   I'm not.

PAUL	You think you got all the right on your side. Well, you don't. You just close your eyes to the truth.
VERNA	Is that so?
PAUL	Darcy and Greg wanna get married.
VERNA	They're not getting married, Paul. Not this summer.
PAUL	They wanna get married now, not when you think it's right. They got their minds made up.
VERNA	They can just unmake them.
PAUL	We could fix up the old folks' place for them.
VERNA	What? Nobody's lived there for ten years.
PAUL	It'd be nice having somebody living on the home place again. You always say it's lonely here.
VERNA	Don't you twist my words.
PAUL	Anyway, it's not in such bad shape. I had a look not too long ago.
VERNA	Paul, no. They've got nothing to live on and no prospects of getting it.
PAUL	Didn't stop us.
VERNA	Things have changed since then. We don't even know if we'll be here next year.
PAUL	Where the hell else would we be?
VERNA	Farming doesn't work any more. It doesn't work for us, and it's not going to work for the children.
PAUL	Don't call them children. They can do anything we do.

VERNA	Sure, like all farm kids. They learn the job before they're old enough to think about it. If you took one generation of farm kids and raised them in town, that would be it for farming.
PAUL	Why would we do that? Farming's still a good life.
VERNA	No. We spend our lives raising food for city people, and they don't know we exist. They think we're a bunch of hillbillies.
PAUL	I don't give a damn what city people think. Sure, things are tough. But we built this house ourselves. We've ridden over every acre of this land.
VERNA	So?
PAUL	I know you liked it too. You used to make me walk with you in the spring to see the crocuses.
VERNA	Yes, I thought they were pretty. Now a field of crocuses just means a dry spring and poor pastures.
PAUL	It means the same as it did when we were young. You're the one that's changed. (*gently turns her toward the hills*) Verna, look. That line of hills? That's part of me. And the shape of that sky. I know that sky. I don't want another one. Look at it.
VERNA	I can't live here just for the sky. I'm sick of this life. Always fighting to get ahead ... always ending up further behind. Having your hopes smashed too many times. Saying "next year" till the words turn bitter in your mouth.
PAUL	You think I've never felt that?
VERNA	I'm not twenty years old any more. I'm afraid.
PAUL	Well ... I'm afraid too. Sometimes I'm scared as a little kid.

VERNA   Why didn't you tell me?

PAUL   I don't know.

VERNA   There has to be something between us ... something we know for sure. Or I can't stand the bad things.

PAUL   I want to talk to you.

VERNA   You used to.... Look, it's time for supper.

PAUL   This is more important. Verna, you've been acting like I've done something you can't forgive. How can that be? I've never done anything so bad.

VERNA hesitates. DARCY enters, down right.

VERNA   Darcy, you are not getting married.

PAUL   Verna, she's been trying to tell you ... she's gonna have a baby. That's why she doesn't want to wait.

VERNA   A baby.

PAUL   Now, Verna...

VERNA   You did it on purpose.

DARCY   Mom, for God's sake.

VERNA   Damn it all. Damn it to hell.

PAUL   Verna, it'll be all right.

VERNA   You knew about this? You knew.

PAUL   No! Darcy just told me.

VERNA   *(to DARCY)* You'll throw it all away. Everything I wanted for you.

DARCY   I can't just do what you want.

VERNA	It's the oldest damn story in the world, isn't it? God, you must think I'm stupid.
DARCY	I don't think you're stupid.
VERNA	You did do it on purpose. Didn't you?
DARCY	Yes.
VERNA	Why, for God's sake? You could get married any time. You could have a baby any time. Darcy, you're so young.
DARCY	I'm not your baby any more, Verna.
VERNA	You don't know what you're doing.
DARCY	I do too.
VERNA	You'll have no life outside the farm but you'll be treated as if you don't count at all.
DARCY	I'll be treated like a farmer.
VERNA	You won't be the farmer. You'll be the farmer's wife.
DARCY	I'll be the farmer and the farmer's wife.
VERNA	You're dreaming.
DARCY	You can't stop me.
VERNA	No.
PAUL	It'll work out. Maybe not like you planned, but it'll work out.
VERNA	I wanted you to have a chance for some dignity.
DARCY	I will.
PAUL	Damn it, Verna, she'll have that.

VERNA	Like I did, I suppose.
PAUL	I thought you did.
VERNA	Because you don't think. If something works for you, you think it must work for me too.
PAUL	What do you mean?
VERNA	I mean that a woman's contribution is not looked at the same way as a man's. Even if she's doing the same work. Are you telling me you don't know that?
PAUL	I don't think I do.
VERNA	Darcy, are you telling me you don't know? You know, all right.

DARCY won't answer.

	We're a little bit inferior. A little bit of a joke. Oh, look at Verna, she combined this whole great big wheat field all by herself.
PAUL	Verna, I've never said that.
VERNA	If we say something, it isn't noticed. If we do something, it must be easy. It must be less important. Like having a baby. Any fool could do that.
DARCY	Oh, for heaven's sake.
PAUL	I've never said that.
VERNA	Any fool could clean a house or look after kids. I mean, some city people think you should get paid for stuff like that. Can you imagine?
PAUL	Would you slow down. I can't keep up with this.
VERNA	Damn it, I will say this. I will figure it out. I have to make you see.

PAUL   I heard what you said, but damn it, it's just a way of talking. It doesn't mean anything.

VERNA   It does. It does mean something. It means we don't count for as much. The men don't think so, and after a while, neither do we.

PAUL   How can it matter that much?

VERNA   I don't know, but it does.

PAUL   Maybe it's been like you say, I don't know. But things are changing.

DARCY   That's right. It'll be different for me.

VERNA   No! You'll spend your life working as hard as any man—

DARCY   Mom—

VERNA   And never once will you hear it said that a woman is as good as a man.

PAUL   But that goes without saying.

VERNA   Does it? If it goes without saying, I'd like to hear you say it. Just once.

PAUL   All right. Women...

                VERNA keeps looking at him.

                Women are just as good as men.

VERNA   My God. You said it.

PAUL   Sure I did. I couldn't have worked here all these years on my own. I know that. I ... appreciate the work you've done.

                VERNA can't answer right away.

                Darcy, go on up to the house.

DARCY	What? Oh ... all right.
	DARCY goes up to house.
PAUL	Well? What are we gonna do?
VERNA	I don't know.
PAUL	I'm trying to understand what you're saying. I could try to be more like what you want. Maybe that's not enough any more, I don't know... I'd like to go on if you would.
VERNA	I'd like to be back where we used to be ... a long time ago. Maybe there's no way back.
PAUL	How could we be like we were then? We lost a child. We raised a child. All the work we did ... thirty years of it.
VERNA	You mean we're no longer the same people?
PAUL	I guess they're still there inside us. But we know more now. Those two people didn't know much about anything.
VERNA	So it's better to be middle-aged and beat-up like some old pickup truck?
PAUL	I don't know if it's better. It's just how it is.
VERNA	It took us thirty years to get to this. It doesn't seem like we got very far.
PAUL	Guess that depends where we were trying to go... Vern, there's something else.
VERNA	What?
PAUL	Flint made me an offer.
VERNA	For our ranch? How much?
PAUL	Enough to buy a house in town and get by.

VERNA	My God, I didn't know anyone would want it.
PAUL	He wants it, all right. In fact, he'd hire me to help work the place. Just think — fifty years old, and my first regular job.
VERNA	You mean we could just stay on here? It might not be all that different. We could live pretty much the same.
PAUL	We'd have to live in town.
VERNA	Why couldn't we live here?
PAUL	He wouldn't be keeping the yard and buildings. It'd just be a few wheat fields and one big pasture.
VERNA	What about our house?
PAUL	Oh, he'd bulldoze and burn it. He don't need anyone living on the place.
VERNA	Why does he want it?
PAUL	It joins up to one corner of his land, and it's got a good spring, which he doesn't have. And then of course, it's *there*.
VERNA	What did you tell him?
PAUL	Told him we'd talk about it.
VERNA	You said that?
PAUL	Yeah. What did you think? That I wouldn't even talk to you?
VERNA	No...
PAUL	He wants an answer pretty quick. If he doesn't get this, he's gonna bid on the Jacksons' place. I guess Jackson already approached him.
VERNA	So what's holding him back?

PAUL	Guess he'd rather have this.
VERNA	So you could live in town and work out here?
PAUL	Or look for some other kind of work.
VERNA	Like what?
PAUL	I don't know. What do you say, Vern? It's what you want, eh?
VERNA	You want me to answer right now?
PAUL	Flint's ready to deal.
VERNA	He'd take down the house? (*PAUL nods*) Dan and Trandafira's place too?
PAUL	Pretty well goes without saying.
VERNA	But you wanted the kids to live there.
PAUL	Yeah. But I gotta admit, this is probably the best offer we'd ever get... Well?
VERNA	We could get clear of all that debt.
PAUL	Yeah.
VERNA	I wonder if anyone would notice ... if we just went away, if there was no one left on the land ... just Harvey and his big machines.
PAUL	So you wanna take the offer?
	VERNA pauses.
VERNA	No. I won't sell that man the farm.
PAUL	Okay, then.
VERNA	What about us?

PAUL   I know we might have to sell some time. I tried not to see it, but I know, all right. I even tried to think of other jobs I could do. I thought maybe I could be a welder or a trucker. If we could just try a couple more years. Then if it's not working, maybe we'd have to sell... I don't wanna leave this place. But I guess I won't die for it either.

      Just think, we might end up being city people ourselves some day... I'm sorry it's been so hard. It's not what I hoped it would be.

VERNA   Nobody could have done more than you did.

PAUL   About Darcy. I wish they'd have waited too.

VERNA   Like they say, eh, "If you could be seventeen again, knowing what you know now."

PAUL   Forty-eight's not so old, you know.

VERNA   No.

PAUL   We're not finished yet, not by a long ways.

VERNA   Not finished with each other?

PAUL   No.

VERNA   We'll give it a try?

PAUL   Yeah... See how it goes.

VERNA   Yeah.

***

The Fruit Machine

by Brian Drader

*The Fruit Machine is a play about growing up and coming to
terms with who you are. The story weaves two times lines—
one in the 60s and the other contemporary. The 90s story
lines centres on an out gay man in his thirties, Peter, who is
still in love with his best friend of years ago, Don, who is
straight.*

> *PETER is making a tape for his friend, DON. He
> pushes the record button on the stereo, to which a
> microphone is attached.*

PETER

So I got fucked out in Edmonton ... *quelle surprise*. He was a
beautiful looking guy ... from New Zealand ... the kind of looks you
want to walk up to and say "Fuck me if I'm wrong, but haven't we
met before"... very fine looking man. With an accent.

I was at the bar .... he picked *me* up. Well, I guess I made myself
pretty obvious, but technically he picked me up. It was great sex.
Great sex. Sex in a really nice hotel room is always great. You don't
have to worry about messing up the place. Anyway, I fell in love.

Really. I did. He touched my penis, I fell in love. Go figure.

Silence.

Sorry. I was just having my own little private Idaho there. So, the
New Zealand guy. The next morning, we're having coffee, making
small talk, blah blah blah, he says he'll see me at The Roost on
Friday night. Mistake ... I've got two days to think about it, right? By
the time Friday rolls around we've already gotten a divorce and
we're fighting over who gets the house, in my head anyway. So I

don't even want to see him anymore, but I go, and he's there, and we go back to his hotel again and have it off and that's it, I'm hooked. Like a fucking fish. I'm hooked. We're married, right? So, it's Saturday morning and I start hinting around that maybe we should get together again that night, or even spend the day together and he starts coming up with all this evasive shit about meeting friends and seeing family, and you won't believe this, Don ... I start to cry. I don't even know the guy and I start to cry because he's going to have dinner with his parents. So there goes my winter in New Zealand, right?

I made him give me a picture of him. I mean I really made him give me one. I wouldn't leave without it. I was pathetic. So he gave me one of his reject passport photos just to get rid of me.

Every time I go back home it ends up like that. I turn into some kind of idiot.

I still call Edmonton home. Weird, eh? I've been living in Winnipeg for almost ten years now. I guess it's because Mom still lives out there.

Okay, so it's Saturday morning, I've been dumped, and I go back to my Mom's new place where I'm staying and the asshole boyfriend starts in on me about where have I been all night. I'm thirty years old, for fuck sake, I don't know him from Adam's sack and he's bitching at me because I didn't come home last night. Yeah, right. So I told him to fuck off, and I started crying again, right in front of him, I have no idea why, and he calls me a faggot and my Mom just stands there, she doesn't say anything, so I say fuck it, that's it, that's the last time I'm going back there, and I threw everything in the van and left. And I meant it, too. That's it. That's the last time. He's a fucking asshole ... a good-for-nothing fucking asshole. I hate his guts.

Silence.

Well. This is pleasant.

Say hi to Beth for me, okay? I cannot believe she hasn't left you yet. Five years. It makes me queasy.

You would have been better off with me, you know that, eh?
Fuck, Beth would have been better off with me. Maybe the three of
us should get together. Can I move in? What do you think ... Pee
break.

*He puts on the Velvet Underground's "Walk on
the Wild Side", sits, and listens.*

***

Lucky Four

by Caroline Russell-King

Lucky Four is a mixed-genre play about two couples. One lives in Calgary, the other, half way around the world. By chance their worlds intersect and a life is saved. They are the lucky four.

ANGELO

I'll go first. I thought of it this morning, but saved it for now. And when I've had my turn, you'll come up with something better, and win. You always do. Do you want to guess what mine is? It's so simple. Come on, guess. Come on, come on. (*pause*) No drugs, no liquor, no women, no cars — an orange. Just one, maybe two. One to tear open and dive into, ripping off the peel, biting into the flesh, feeling the juice exploding every taste bud in my mouth. The second to savour. First smelling the delicate peel, feeling the texture of the little craters in the skin, memorizing the little green star plugging the end and slowly, every so slowly, piercing the skin with my thumbnail, releasing that bitter odour that makes the glands on the sides of your tongue secrete. This is a fantasy. I have clean hands. Slowly I coax the peel from the fruit to reveal the blankety white until it is unclothed, naked. Now I am going to violate it. I stick the same offending thumb down into the heart of it, tearing it apart, exposing the segments which cocoon the pips. I gently pry one segment, tearing it away from the others, and put it up to my lips. My tongue caresses the soft texture of the outside, then I employ the teeth which bear pressure until it can withhold no longer and the juice squirts to the roof of my mouth. Another bite saturates my gums and teeth in the most exquisite sweetness.

***

Comfort and Joy

by Kelley Jo Burke

MARGARET, a forty-ish woman, sits with her son and daughter, on Christmas Eve, in her daughter's room. Her daughter has spent months in her room, preparing for this night. It is now wonderfully and fearfully decorated for Christmas. They are waiting for the father of the family to come home. MARGARET has been drinking.

MARGARET

I threw all mine out, you know. All my gorgeous stuff. My granny's Sacred Heart. My rosary. Real jet and garnet beads, blessed by the archbishop himself. Right in the trash. I had one of those pictures, you know, where you look at him one way, and he's dead, and then another, and he's risen. I loved that. Him opening his eyes, to me. (*drinking*) I almost pulled that out of the dustbin. But it was a Friday, and so by the time I got there, Dad had puked half his pay cheque on it, and it was all soggy, and the eye thing didn't work—

I know what you do in here. I did it too. Must run in the family. Stupidity. Fifteen. Should have been smoking, and losing my knickers in somebody's DeSoto. But what did I do? Filled my room with gorgeous stuff, and lay on my bed, dreaming of Jesus.

He was a looker. Our Jesus. So ... heavy. Hands and feet tearing with the weight of him. Down he'd go, those fine hard legs all smashed to plaster dust.

I wanted to be perfect ... perfect enough to help. Get him off that fucking cross, take his face in my lap, and hear him whisper "Thank you Mary Margaret. It's easier now." But I wasn't fit to touch his bloody feet.

So I gave up sweets. I slept on the floor, without a pillow. I washed eight, ten times a day, God, with bars of Sunlight Soap and flannel. And I was ... scrawny, stiff, and covered head to toe in rash. I reeked of the odour of sanctity. I thought ... I might. You know. One night. I might creep in. And touch his feet.

And then I got my period.

My mother, God bless her, my mother was a not a tender woman. Not a "What's troubling you dear? Oh Mom sometimes I just don't feel fresh", sort of woman. No, by God. She took one look at my sobbing self, wiped my legs with a sock from the rag bag, and pointed to the instructions on the Kotex box..

I couldn't go back to chapel, could I? See him, hanging there, waiting, and hands and feet ripping to shit, and me not fit to do a thing about it.

I was hairy and bloody and bulgier everyday. He'd have scrabbled up the cross to get away from me, the Holy Mother fending me off with the Babe as a billy club. I'd of started an iconic riot.

If only you could reason with the man.

"Sweetheart. Get down. Tell them it's a misunderstanding. We'll get some Dettol on those cuts. There's no saying but with some physio we could get you out of this godforsaken death hole and off to Alexandria, or Crete. Someplace people can take a joke."

He could fish, he could herd sheep, he was good with his hands. All and all, I think your grandmother would have approved.

But I'm telling you, girl, he wasn't coming down. Not for me. Not for you. My theory is, he likes it up there.

***

House of Sacred Cows

by Padma Viswananthan

*ANAND is a graduate student from India. The ghosts of his
parents, who died just before he left for Canada, have waited
two years for him to finish his M.A. and return to India to
arrange his sisters' marriages and settle down. They are
shocked now to find he has not finished his M.A. and, no
longer having university housing, has moved into a co-ed co-
op. Most of their discussions in the play are about these
matters, but in this scene, they are just paying a visit.*

> *ANAND goes up to his room with luggage and
> sandwich. He puts away things, takes out an
> Indian movie magazine and eats while reading.
> After he has enjoyed this for a minute or so,
> AMMA and APPA appear to some austere
> Carnatic music.*

AMMA   Oh, Anand, what are you eating?

ANAND   A sandwich, Amma.

AMMA   Remember what I said would happen if you eat
            meat.

ANAND   Oh, I remember, Amma.

AMMA   My only son must not reincarnate as a pig.

ANAND   Even Vishnu had one avatar as wild boar, Amma.

APPA   A bore! But we tolerated. Such a perennial bore.

ANAND   Perennial, yes — what of vegetables? Eating
            vegetable life must equally be an act of evil.

AMMA	No, no, no. Plants are there for eating only.
ANAND	What if I came back as a squash or a pea plant, Amma?
AMMA	Doesn't happen.
ANAND	Then animals. Other castes eat animals, animals eat other animals.
AMMA	Are you a child to ask such questions, Anand?
ANAND	Even great Guru Nanak says "We are born from flesh, we suckle at flesh, and as flesh we die and decay ... why shun the flesh?"
AMMA	You can quote sardarji to me!? You are converting to be a Sikh?
ANAND	No Amma, no, no, no... (*looking longingly at sandwich and reading material*)
AMMA	I only fed you, I only nursed you when you were a this big baby. Let them go and do all every filthy, filthy thing. I am telling you.
ANAND	We must consume life to live. This results in accumulation of karma, but it is a necessary evil.
APPA	The necessary evil. But they employed us and gave us pants to wear.
AMMA	Show me the sandwich, Anand.
ANAND	Amma!
AMMA	Show it. (*ANAND obeys*) Meat! Meat!
APPA	"The poor benighted Hindoo / He does the best he kin do / Sticks to his caste / From first to last / And for trousers just lets his skin do." Kipling couldn't have said it better.

ANAND   Amma, no, Amma, this is some ... imitation, made from soybeans and colourings, to look and taste like meat.

AMMA   Why?

ANAND   I don't know. (*looks at sandwich, offers it*) Bite?

AMMA   *Chi!* (*sniffingly rejects his offer*)

                    AMMA and APPA vanish, ANAND sighs, goes to his desk, dips quill, begins writing.

ANAND   The funeral pyre does not address the body. It is a vehicle for transport of the soul. The body is symbolic, a burnt offering. Then again, fire, by following its nature, devours the sticks of wood that gave it life. (*pauses in writing*) So, Agni, god of fire and devoted son, is said to have eaten his parents.

***

Selkirk Avenue

by Bruce McManus

Mary is dying. In their last moments together Harold and Mary try to reconcile their differences and affirm their love by remembering and reinterpreting the past. The scene moves back and forth between the past and present.'

                    Lights up on MARY and HAROLD.

MARY   If we had children.

HAROLD   They would have been very confused.

                    MARY fumbles in her pocket and pulls out a ring.

HAROLD   When you remember too much does it make you young or old?

MARY   They would have been good children.

HAROLD   We could have had children.

MARY   Yes, yes we could have ... if you weren't so stubborn.

HAROLD   Principles. I had principles.

MARY   Everybody in the North End has principles.

HAROLD   You were stubborn. I had principles.

MARY   Help me, Harold.

HAROLD   Are you dying?

MARY   Not yet.

HAROLD Good. It's against health regulations. No one can die in a photo studio.

MARY   I can't get my rings on. My hands won't work anymore.

        HAROLD stands and approaches MARY.

        My mother's ring. I can't get it on.

HAROLD You're helpless then?

MARY   I'm helpless before you.

HAROLD (*pause*) I never had another woman.

MARY   (*laughing*) Don't be silly.

HAROLD It's true. You were my last woman.

MARY   That's a bare-faced lie.

HAROLD (*pause*) You were the only woman that counted.

MARY   And you were counting?

HAROLD There's no reason to be insulting.

MARY   No ... no, help me with this.

        HAROLD takes the ring from MARY.

HAROLD A wedding ring.

MARY   My mother's. (*holding out her hand, wedding finger forward*)

HAROLD (*not moving*) You came here to get help with your rings?

MARY   You remember the Silvers?

HAROLD	Of course I do. I have a perfect memory.
MARY	You're still in good shape for an old man.
HAROLD	Thirty years, Mary.
MARY	Anger kept me alive.
HAROLD	You're not angry anymore.
MARY	Put the ring on, you old fool.

> *HAROLD reaches for MARY's right hand. She pulls it away, holding out her left. ISRAEL sits at the table. HAROLD takes his camera suitable to the Thirties and heads to the SILVERS. All the while...*

HAROLD	I remember the Silvers ... why wouldn't I remember the Silvers? I'm not that old.

> *The SILVERS enter.*

MARY	Harold ...
HAROLD	I came as soon as I could.
ISRAEL	You brought your camera.
HAROLD	At your service.
ISRAEL	Good.

> *Silence for a moment.*

HAROLD	I thought this was an emergency.
ISRAEL	And how would you define an emergency?
HAROLD	Birth? Disaster?
ISRAEL	A phone call in the night? A taxi at the door. God forbid, a telegram?

HAROLD	Death?
ISRAEL	Miriam is well.
HAROLD	Thank God.
MARY	(*to Harold*) Your legs were so skinny, Harold.
HAROLD	(*to MARY*) Skinny legs? You thought I had skinny legs?
MARY	They were so thin.
HAROLD	My legs held me up. What else do you want?
ISRAEL	This is a woman emergency.
HAROLD	All those years, you thought I had skinny legs.
MARY	I would have fattened you up, Harold.
ISRAEL	Death is not an emergency to women.
HAROLD	And what then, Mr. Israel Wisdom, am I doing here with my camera?
ISRAEL	What do you usually do with a camera?
MARY	You always looked through those cameras so you didn't have to see anything.

MIRIAM enters, smiling.

HAROLD	Mrs. Silver, beautiful as always.
MARY	And you were such a flirt.
MIRIAM	Thank you for coming, Harold.
HAROLD	You're welcome ... perhaps you will tell me why I'm here.
ISRAEL	We need a photographer.

MARY   She looked absolutely beautiful.

                Enter YETTA in her wedding dress.

HAROLD   This looks like a wedding dress.

ISRAEL   See Miriam, we hired the right man.

HAROLD   Mazeltov, Yetta. (*setting up his camera*)

ISRAEL   And he speaks Yiddish, too ...

YETTA   Mother, does it look alright?

MIRIAM   You look like a queen.

                MIRIAM readjusts the dress, YETTA poses,
                ISRAEL watches proudly.

HAROLD   It was a satin dress ...

MARY   Silk, Harold. With lace.

HAROLD   Satin; no one could afford silk.

MARY   Silk. Everybody knew Yetta Silver got married in a
                silk dress. She was the only girl in the North End
                who had a silk wedding dress.

YETTA   Do I look alright, Harold?

HAROLD   Beautiful. (*taking the picture*)

MARY   You could never resist a beautiful woman.

HAROLD   Tell me Israel, how could a man like you lose.

ISRAEL   I asked myself that, Harold. How could a man like
                me lose?

YETTA   You couldn't lose, Father. You just couldn't.

                HAROLD packs up his camera, and heads back to
                his studio. Meanwhile ...

MARY	Envy is a sin. But even God would let you envy a woman who got married in a silk wedding dress in 1938.
HAROLD	1939. A satin wedding dress.
MARY	Silk.

Lights down on the SILVERS, they exit.

MARY	I helped Mrs. Chornopyski sew the lace.
HAROLD	I've got pictures here ... satin.
MARY	That was a wedding.
HAROLD	I have pictures here ... somewhere.
MARY	Put my ring on, Harold.
HAROLD	I have no pictures of you. Do you know that?
MARY	I don't feel right without my ring.
HAROLD	You always moved. You wouldn't keep quiet and you wouldn't keep still.
MARY	My ring.

HAROLD approaches MARY with the ring.

HAROLD	This means nothing, Mary.
MARY	A man like you doesn't need superstitions. (*holding out her hand*)
HAROLD	This means nothing. I'm doing an old lady a favour.
MARY	Don't be a silly old man.
HAROLD	(*struggling to put the ring on her finger*) You've got old lady fingers.
MARY	With this ring I thee wed.

HAROLD	Mary Lobchuk ... don't fool now. I don't like that smile, Mary. Mary? Why are you smiling like that?
MARY	It's nothing.
HAROLD	You made the choices here. You. I did what had to be done. I was true to myself.
MARY	Yes, Harold.
HAROLD	Yes, Harold. (*alarmed*) Don't say "Yes, Harold." Mary, should I get the doctor?
MARY	No dear.
HAROLD	My God. Mary, don't die ... listen, I love you.
MARY	Yes.
HAROLD	I do. I love you ... Mary?
MARY	I know.
HAROLD	You can't die ... we have a number of things to discuss.
MARY	Oh shut up.
HAROLD	Your arrogance, for instance.
MARY	I love you.
HAROLD	Only you would tell me to shut up. You come in here after thirty years ... you tell me to shut up. Thirty ... fifty years of acting as if your every idea and thought came from a higher source. Your God. There's no need for that, Mary. Man is enough. There is no need. There is no need ...

He walks to her and strokes her cheek. Lights down.

***

Children of Neon Lights

by Bettina Grassmann

*Jeremy and Nicole are committed to a psyche ward the night
the Gulf War began. Jeremy is deeply depressed, and has
been trying to slit his wrists all night, but the wildly manic
Nicole keeps interrupting. Finally, Jeremy answers his own
question, "Why?"*

JEREMY

Oh well. We're actually quite big. We played at Amigos a coupla
times, and —well — I had a girlfriend even. Jill — met her this
summer. Everything's great, okay? Everyday I go to class, go to
Louis' for lunch, go to a band practice or study or something. Every
weekend get tanked up at Amigos, take my girlfriend out.
Everything's great, okay? Playing with my band. And I'm loving it,
right? 'Cause I'm on top, with all those girls, screaming, thinking I'm
so hot because I can stand on a stage and sing out of key into a mike.
My girlfriend, she fuckin' worshipped me. Loved to show me off. Like
I matched her clothes. Really-pseudo hippie, okay? Everything's
great, okay? Everything's cool. And then one night I'm at Amigos.
It's got that hazy sort of glow, the after-two-a.m.-and-six-beers glow.
And there's this obnoxious red light flashing on and off. On and off.
And so it occurs to me. We're having this really great time because
that light is flashing. And in 20 minutes, they'll turn that light off,
and this'll all be gone, and we'll go home. Just like we're supposed
to. Okay, so — I wanna tell someone this, this new revelation. Look
for my girl. And she's dressed really hot, right, in this red tank top,
and Docs, and she's doing this sort of dance, some kind of grunge
polka, like this (*imitates her*). Then she turns to me, and goes "Isn't
this cool?" Suddenly, my girlfriend turned into an android.
Mechanical. And suddenly, I don't know why I'm going to school, or
playing in a band, or dating her. Maybe there was something I
believed in once, something I knew. Maybe a neon light shut on
somewhere and told me "Go to school" "Join a band". I don't know.

It's all just a light that switched on, and I responded. So I died. It happened slowly. But I numbed out — gradually, I feel nothing. I think nothing. When those lights switch on I don't feel anything.

***

fareWel

by Ian Ross

With the failure of the welfare cheques to appear, Teddy decides to pursue his own brand of self-government. Using the reserve's restaurant-convenience store-coffee shop-gas station, he calls a meeting to take control of the reserve and its future.

> *Lights come up on Walter's Restaurant. TEDDY has arranged some chairs, which await an audience. A wooden Pepsi box is being used as a podium. There are some crude signs with pictures of TEDDY on them. NIGGER hobbles towards the counter, dragging his 'crutch', and uses whatever he can to prop himself up.*

NIGGER   Hey, Walter. Walter. Where the hell are you? I need some med-cin. Fix my tooth for me. And my leg too. This stupid stick hurts my arm. (*throwing down the 'crutch'*) Where the hell is Walter?

> *TEDDY enters.*

TEDDY   O.K. Come sit over here. (*motioning to the chairs*)

NIGGER   I can't walk good.

TEDDY   Be a man, eh?

NIGGER   O.K. Wait.

> *NIGGER grabs some chips, then hobbles over to the chairs and sits down.*

NIGGER   What's this anyways?

TEDDY   It's a meeting. You'll see when Melvin and them
                   get here.

                   ROBERT walks in.

TEDDY   Shit.

NIGGER   What?

TEDDY   We don't need this asshole.

ROBERT   Walter? Walter? Teddy have you seen Walter?

TEDDY   Nope.

                   *ROBERT walks behind the counter and pulls out a
                   little book.*

ROBERT   Tell Walter I came to pay my bill and left this
                   cheque for him. (*ROBERT looks in the book and puts
                   a cheque in it*) Nine hundred bucks. Man. Man.
                   Those kids'll make me go broke. Tell Walter not to
                   let my kids charge burgers and stuff on here again
                   unless I say it's O.K. Alright?

TEDDY   Tell him yourself.

                   MELVIN walks in with RACHEL and PHYLLIS.

TEDDY   Ahhh shit. Melvin I told you just to bring men.

MELVIN   I didn't bring them. They came here by themself.

TEDDY   Where's Cheezie and Rudy and those guys. I told
                   you to bring them.

MELVIN   Cheezie's passed out and those other guys went to
                   Little Sask for bingo.

TEDDY   For fuck sakes.

RACHEL   You're such a little shit Teddy. Just 'cause you hear
                   I call a meeting and so you have to call one?

TEDDY	I called this meeting before you did.
RACHEL	Let's ask Walter. Walter? Walter. Where the hell's Walter?
TEDDY	He's pumping gas.
RACHEL	It doesn't matter anyways. I called this meeting first.
ROBERT	What meeting?
RACHEL	The one I set up to fix this problem with welfare.
TEDDY	That's what this meeting's about.
RACHEL	Good. Then we'll be talking about the same thing.
TEDDY	No. This is my meeting.
PHYLLIS	This is our meeting, Teddy.
TEDDY	No. This is mine. No women.
RACHEL	She doesn't mean just us. She means all of us here.
TEDDY	We don't need women involved in this political process.
ROBERT	What political process? What are you guys talking about?
RACHEL	We're gonna talk about what this reserve's gonna do now that there's no more fareWel.
ROBERT	What?
NIGGER	No fareWel cheques today. No happy day. It was sad day today.
TEDDY	You're not gonna talk about anything, Rachel. You get the hell out of here.
RACHEL	No. Why don't you get the hell out of here, Teddy. No one asked you to do this.

TEDDY	And no one asked you.
ROBERT	What are you doing? What are you guys talking about?

RACHEL and TEDDY speak at the same time.

RACHEL	Teaching.
TEDDY	Self-government.

RACHEL and ROBERT speak at the same time.

BOTH	What?
TEDDY	This is about self-government.
RACHEL	Whose self-government?
TEDDY	Ours. The Partridge Crop First Nation's.
MELVIN	This reserve?
TEDDY	It's a nation now. A new name for a new power.
PHYLLIS	You want to talk about self-government?
TEDDY	I'm gonna do it.
ROBERT	The Chief isn't going to let you.
TEDDY	He doesn't care. If he did he would have got our cheques for us. Right? Right, Phyllis?
PHYLLIS	I dunno.
TEDDY	He's not even here.
ROBERT	Where is he?
ALL	(*except ROBERT*) He's in Vegas.
ROBERT	Oh. Nobody told me.

RACHEL	You can't have self-government here, Teddy. No one wants it. They just want their welfare and parties.
TEDDY	That's what you want. I want a new future for our people.
RACHEL	And our people's money. How do you suppose to do this anyways?
TEDDY	We'll have nominations and then pick the Chief. I call this meeting to order. You guys sit down.

RACHEL and ROBERT stand. MELVIN and PHYLLIS move to sit down. TEDDY stops PHYLLIS.

TEDDY	Not you.
PHYLLIS	Why?
TEDDY	You're a woman.
RACHEL	So?
TEDDY	Go make food for Schmidty's wake.
RACHEL	Go make another baby.
TEDDY	Hey. We don't need you here.
ROBERT	You need everybody, Teddy.
TEDDY	Not women.
PHYLLIS	Let's go, Rachel.

PHYLLIS tries to move RACHEL. RACHEL doesn't move.

ROBERT	Let them stay, Teddy. Future chiefs are fair.
TEDDY	Stay or go. I don't care. They don't get a vote. I call this meeting to order.

RACHEL	Who died and made you Chief?
TEDDY	No one. Yet.
ROBERT	Are you the chair?
TEDDY	Yes.
NIGGER	Maybe he's a table.
TEDDY	Shut up, Nigger. Who nominates me?
ROBERT	Hold it, Teddy. You should be chosen chair first. And someone has to second that nomination. But you should have the selection of chair first.
NIGGER	How come all this furniture?
TEDDY	That's white man's ways.
RACHEL	The whole thing you're doing is white man's ways. We never used to vote for Chief.
TEDDY	And women weren't allowed.
ROBERT	Hold it. Hold it. You guys can't do this. You need to talk about this. Talk about it more.
RACHEL	Yes. Talk, then do something.
TEDDY	That's all we've been doing is talk. It's time to move.
ROBERT	You need to consult the elders. Like Sheldon here.
TEDDY	Who? Nigger? (*TEDDY starts laughing*)
RACHEL	Not consult. Teach. We need to ask them to teach us.
TEDDY	We need you to shut up.
PHYLLIS	We need help. Robert, help us.

ROBERT	I'd be wasting my time.
TEDDY	If that's what you think self-government is, get the hell out.

ROBERT waits and is about to leave.

MELVIN	You'd be a good Chief, Robert.
TEDDY	Shut up, you little asshole.
MELVIN	I'd even vote for you for free.

ROBERT stays.

ROBERT	Go ahead, Teddy, nominate yourself.
TEDDY	I nominate myself Chief of the Partridge Crop First Nation.
ROBERT	O.K. now someone has to second it, or else you can't stand.
NIGGER	Why? Does he have to sit down?
ROBERT	You. Melvin. Do you second Teddy for Chief?
MELVIN	I do.
ROBERT	O.K. Well?
MELVIN	Well what?
ROBERT	Say, "I second Teddy for Chief."
MELVIN	Oh. I second Teddy for Chief.
NIGGER	I third him.
ROBERT	You can't do that.
NIGGER	Why?

ROBERT	You don't have to. Now you have to have other nominations for the same position.
RACHEL	I nominate myself for Chief.
TEDDY	You can't.
RACHEL	I just did.
MELVIN	I nominate Robert Traverse for Chief.
RACHEL	Second me, Phyllis.
NIGGER	I nominate me for Chief.
PHYLLIS	I second Rachel for Chief.
RACHEL	I second Robert for Chief.
TEDDY	Stop.
ROBERT	Yes. Hold on. Thank you, but I don't want to be Chief. Don't nominate me. I'm not standing.
NIGGER	Standing. Sitting. Chairs. Tables. First. Second. How come Robert knows so much. I bet he's just lying to us.
ROBERT	I'm not lying to you. You can look it up. The rules I'm using are called *Robert's Rules of Order.*
NIGGER	Aaaahhh. See. I knew it. These are his rules. He's just trying to get what he wants.
ROBERT	They're not mine.
NIGGER	Why are they called Robert's rules then?
ROBERT	I don't know. Because that's who wrote them.
NIGGER	Aaaahhh. He's lying. He wrote them.
ROBERT	I learned them doing community development for Indian Affairs.

NIGGER	He's lying.
TEDDY	Shut up, Nigger.
NIGGER	We're supposed to sing "O Canada" before our meeting or "God Save the Queen".
TEDDY & ROBERT	Shut up, Nigger.
NIGGER	(*singing*) O Canada. Our home and native land (*punching up 'native' for added effect*) A native person wrote that song.
MELVIN	That's not what it means.
NIGGER	Sure it does. Native. That's us right.
MELVIN	Yeah, but not like that.
NIGGER	I read a book. It said Canada is from Natives. It means "free land".
TEDDY	Shut up, you assholes. I disbar Robert as Chief.
NIGGER	I second that.
PHYLLIS	You guys can't do that.
RACHEL	What a fuckin' joke. Robert's right. You don't even know what you're doing, Teddy.
TEDDY	At least I'm doing something.
RACHEL	Nobody asked you.
ROBERT	Hey. Hey. It doesn't matter. I'm not standing. I mean I'm not accepting the nomination for Chief. So you have nothing to worry about.
MELVIN	Can you do that?
ROBERT	Yes.

MELVIN	Oh.
PHYLLIS	I nominate Melvin.
TEDDY & RACHEL	I second.
TEDDY	I second him.
RACHEL	I do.
ROBERT	You guys. You guys. This isn't how you do it.
NIGGER	How do you know?
ROBERT	Because I've been to meetings. I know how to do this. Be quiet. Look. Listen. You need a secretary. You need more people. You can't do this the way you're doing it. Planning. Preparation. You need all of these things. These things have to be thought out.
TEDDY	Why?
ROBERT	Ah hell, I'm leaving. You people are hopeless.
MELVIN	(*stopping him*) Wait. Robert you have to help us. You know the rules.
ROBERT	These guys aren't even listening to me. We can't do this. This doesn't mean anything.
TEDDY	Let him go.
MELVIN	Just stay.
ROBERT	There's no use. This isn't gonna work. We have to know what we're doing first.
MELVIN	Maybe. But still help us.
TEDDY	Stay or go. I don't give a shit. It's gonna happen without you.

MELVIN leads him back to a chair.

TEDDY   O.K., now we vote for Chief.

ROBERT   The nominations have to be closed first.

MELVIN   What?

ROBERT   Never mind.

PHYLLIS   Wait. Wait. You have to give a speech.

TEDDY   Oh yeah. Let Melvin speak first.

MELVIN   I want Robert to speak for me.

PHYLLIS   Wait. Wait. I wanna pray first.

TEDDY   No.

PHYLLIS   Come on. I'm not nominated for anything. We need
               to pray first. Our people need God if we're gonna
               have self-government.

TEDDY   Our people need our own religion. Not that
               whiteman bullshit religion.

NIGGER   We need to sing "O Canada".

               *PHYLLIS starts to pray, eventually everyone
               except TEDDY and RACHEL bow their heads.*

TEDDY   Fuckin' women.

PHYLLIS   Oh God, bless us in this thing we're doing, and don't
               let us be failures. And thank you for giving us
               Robert who can tell us what to do. And let our
               leaders be right and good for our people. Thank you
               Jesus. I don't know what self-government is, or what
               it's gonna be, but I pray you'll help us in it. Thank
               you, Jesus. And I'm sorry that we almost smoked
               your Bible and that nothing will happen to Rachel
               for that. Or to me. And don't let there be a number
               three. And bless Nigger, our elder, and Melvin, and
               Teddy. And Lord, maybe this isn't the time for us to
               have self-government, maybe we should wait for—

TEDDY	Amen.
RACHEL	Let her finish.
PHYLLIS	I'm finished. Amen. Jesus. Amen.
TEDDY	O.K. Go and talk, Melvin.
MELVIN	No.
ROBERT	Go on already.
MELVIN	Wait. I want Robert to talk first. I'm not gonna talk. I just want to hear what he has to say.
TEDDY	Ahhh shit. O.K. then. Let's get this over with. Robert's gonna talk first.
ROBERT	I don't wanna talk.

> *RACHEL holds onto the seat of her chair and begins hopping up and down with it, chanting "Talk". Soon, everyone else who is sitting joins in, until ROBERT rises, sits on the box and begins to talk.*

ROBERT	Listen. Self-government is something native people should have had long ago. Instead of begging for handouts. Whether it's for our schools or whatever. A lot of us who don't think we are, are really bums.
NIGGER	That's me. I was a bum on Main Street until that police car hit me and I got ten thousand dollars and I came home, and then I sobered up.
MELVIN	You never sobered up. You're still drunk.
ROBERT	I didn't mean you, Nigger. I was just trying to make a point. I'm sorry if I offended you.
NIGGER	No. That's O.K. I know who I am, and what I was. Just let me say something. The way I used to get money from people on the street was when I looked really pitiful. That's what you guys do when you go

to Ottawa. Look really sad and they'll give you money. (*making a pitiful face*) Or else play music. Like a fiddle. I'm gonna take my fiddle and go back to Winnipeg and make money.

ROBERT   You asked me here for a meeting. A meeting on self-government. What is that? Can any of you tell me?

RACHEL   It's a different name for what we got now.

TEDDY   It's self-government. Just like the words mean. We govern ourselves. No more Indian Affairs.

ROBERT   OK ... and?

TEDDY   And ... we get our own money. We get to look after ourselves.

RACHEL   You mean you get our money.

ROBERT   Rachel. Please. How much money is that, do you think?

TEDDY   A couple million.

ROBERT   Probably. Can you balance books?

TEDDY   Sure.

ROBERT   That wouldn't help you anyways. The Partridge Crop Reserve is broke. Their cheques all bounce. There's only one bank in Ashern that will cash welfare cheques and only welfare cheques. No other reserve cheques.

PHYLLIS   Teddy wouldn't even cash my little cheque.

TEDDY   Shut up, you.

ROBERT   Do you know what a ledger is? Or a balance sheet? Or how to do a payroll? Or calculate taxes?

TEDDY   We don't pay taxes.

ROBERT	Sure we do. We pay GST. Soon we'll be paying income tax too.
NIGGER	No way.
ROBERT	Yes we will. Who do you think pays for your happy day?
TEDDY	The government.
ROBERT	And who gives them money?
TEDDY	I don't know.
ROBERT	Taxpayers. They can't even pay for Medicare anymore. You think they're gonna care about a bunch of Indians?
TEDDY	They owe us.
ROBERT	I know they do. But you live on what they've given you. The land on this reserve is all we're ever gonna get. This reserve is less than a thousand square miles. And this country is millions of square miles. But this is all we're gonna get. And we're gonna get even less, as the money runs out.
TEDDY	We'll just take our land back.
MELVIN	We can't. We lost it. We're a defeated nation.
TEDDY	We're not a defeated nation. We never were. If they came here and kicked our asses instead of shaking our hands everything would have been fine. Then our people understood defeat. What it is to lose a war. And what that means. Instead we get tricked. And all this shit you see around you is because of that. They're still doing it. What do you think fareWel is?
ROBERT	We need self-determination. Not self-government. And. Within the current political system.
TEDDY	That's what we've had for the last hunerd years.

RACHEL   What Robert just tried to do is what we need.
              Teaching.

              RACHEL walks up to and stands on the podium.

TEDDY   Get off there.

RACHEL   We need teaching. We need to learn to live a
              different way. Not on welfare. We can't keep doing
              the same thing over and over. We're only gonna get
              one chance at self-government and we have to
              make it right.

TEDDY   Yeah. Good. O.K.

              TEDDY tries to pull RACHEL off the podium.

RACHEL   Let me finish. We need God too. If you want to
              believe Christian. Fine. If you want to believe
              Traditional. Fine. But we got to stop fighting each
              other all the time.

TEDDY   Yeah. (*TEDDY pulling her off the box*)

RACHEL   And we need to listen to each other. Teddy.

              *ROBERT starts to clap for RACHEL. The others
              join in, except TEDDY. ROBERT starts to leave.*

PHYLLIS   Where are you going, Robert?

ROBERT   Home.

PHYLLIS   How come?

ROBERT   I've seen this one before.

              ROBERT leaves.

TEDDY   O.K. Melvin it's your turn to get up there.

              *MELVIN sits, until TEDDY grabs him and puts
              him at the front. He does not stand on the box.*

MELVIN	I don't know wannu.
TEDDY	Make your speech.
MELVIN	I don't know what a ledger is. And I didn't know our reserve was so small compared to the rest of Canada. Robert should be Chief. Not me. I don't even know why you voted me for Chief, because I can't be Chief. I'm from Dogtown. Even though I'm Bill C-31.
NIGGER	Anyone can be Chief. Even a whiteman.
MELVIN	I'm not white. But I feel Indian.
RACHEL	It's what's in your heart.
MELVIN	I don't know what's in my heart.
TEDDY	Just shut up and finish your speech.
MELVIN	O.K. The only thing I know for sure is that nobody used to want to be Chief. The Indian agent used to come and he would give the Chief a new suit, and the councillors would get nothing.
NIGGER	That's right. I was a councillor for ten years.
MELVIN	The Chief worked free. Now that the Chief and council get paid, everybody wants to be the Chief or on council. Maybe that's what we should have again. I shouldn't be Chief anyways. I sniff.

TEDDY begins clapping, everyone but RACHEL joins in.

TEDDY	(*rising*) That was a good speech, Melvin.
RACHEL	Let him finish.
MELVIN	I'm finished.

TEDDY stands on the box.

TEDDY   Dih na way mahg a nay duk,

MELVIN   Wait, Teddy. Speak English.

TEDDY   Dih na way mahg a nay duk, asa wasa ki bi isha min ooma ka ai ing. Mi ooma ka dasi wo big ai ing. Ki kee asha dis oomin, shigo noong-um aa michi pee ang oki ma wi win chi meeni nang shoonian. A pee woogi mak an wi an ka ween shig o da ashan diki seem. Kakina awiah ta meena shoonian. Ki ka meeni ni nim shoonia. A way woogi mah kan ka ishad Las Vegas, pi san igoo mas kowi see win ki woo ta bi namin. A pee das ta gooshing ki ka sagichi wa binanan, omah woo chi ish koon i ganing. Ki ka machi a tad i minoma. Kakina oono a tagaa wi nan ta pisco wheels of fortune, blackjack, shig oh slot machines. Mi ih kaa ishi shoonia kaa ing. Keena wind ki ga woono dah min awa naan ki anishinabaywid. Ka ween a woshi may ongo blond hair ka ahwad, shi go ka ay kjee wabiwad Bill C-31 ka inid oh, ka pi woo ta pin a wad ki shoonia min nin. Shi go ka iah way anishinabaa wit tau win. Ki ka woo tabi na min iway koy ak anamiahwin. Ka ween a wooshi may owoo wa way miti goo ishi woo dana mi way igamik. Ka Keena Bazooka Joe ta anishinabe wooshi pee I gaday. (*holding up a Bazooka Joe comic*) Keena wah ka kin ah ki masi na a mak wim ka goo. Phyllis ki masi na amau a shoonia. Nigger, ki masi na mow neen ka ki woo tabi na man ki wee bid.

NIGGER   Ka ween koosha ki kee wood tabi na seen ni wee wipid. Ka abi ni wee sa kaa dam.

TEDDY   Melvin ki masi na a mau ka kee weegi nan chi aihin truck, ta goo gravel chi aihin ki meeka nang. Shig oh kaa keen Rachel ki masi na a mow chi pis nanabi ann, chi ki pa aman kidoon.

         RACHEL kicks over an empty chair.

RACHEL   That's a lie.

MELVIN   What?

PHYLLIS	Rachel, don't.
TEDDY	Paa ka aka way hookerish.
RACHEL	I don't owe you anything. He says you owe him for that gravel on your Dad's road, Melvin.
MELVIN	What?
TEDDY	I got you that gravel. You wouldn't even have got any if it wasn't for me. You're a Bill C-31er.
MELVIN	I got that gravel. You didn't... I even asked before you and yet they gave everyone gravel except for me. That's how you can tell who's Bill C-31 on this reserve. They're the ones with dirt on their roads.
TEDDY	That's 'cause you're not pure.
MELVIN	I'm more Indian than you. (*TEDDY laughs*) In my heart. In my heart.
TEDDY	All you got is a card and some bullshit treaty number.
RACHEL	Teddy, you're not even pure yourself. Your granny was part white.
TEDDY	Woo nab in, pisahnabin.
RACHEL	You don't even know what you're doing here. This is a joke. Look at this fuckin' sign with your stupid face on it. (*RACHEL picks up one of the signs*) You look like a fuckin' dog.
TEDDY	Shut up.
RACHEL	We need teaching. That's the only way we're ever gonna get better.
TEDDY	Shut up.
RACHEL	No.

TEDDY	You shut up. Or I'll tell everyone what you are.
RACHEL	Go ahead. You're just as bad.
TEDDY	You know what this slut did?
RACHEL	He sleeps with hookers.
TEDDY	How would you know that?
RACHEL	Because. You were gonna sleep with me.
TEDDY	Yeah, right. One time in Winnipeg, I phone the hooker escort service and tell them to send me over a real pretty one, and this is what they send me.
RACHEL	You're just as bad. You sleep with hookers.
TEDDY	I sure as hell didn't want to sleep with you. I just laughed my head off.
RACHEL	You liar. You chased me down the hall. You wanted me so bad I could see your old pecker through your pants.
TEDDY	Ki ki chi ka wanim aki din.
RACHEL	Ka ween weeka ki da packi di na moosi noon. Why don't you go look after Margret and your baby, instead of making things worse for us.
TEDDY	(*grabbing RACHEL by the hair*) You whore bitch. You'd spread your legs for anyone with money eh? I would never sleep with you. (*releasing her*) She's not even proud of her own hair. Look at it. It's dyed. Indian hair. Black hair. She's embarrassed of it. It isn't even fuckin' clean.
NIGGER	That's enough.
TEDDY	You're damn right it's enough.

> *TEDDY pushes RACHEL towards the door and kicks her in the rear.*

You get the hell off my reserve and get your black ass home.

MELVIN sits, lost.

PHYLLIS   You're gonna get it, Teddy.

TEDDY   Maybe you're the one who's gonna get it, Phyllis.

PHYLLIS helps RACHEL, and they both leave.

NIGGER   Why'd you do that, Teddy?

TEDDY   Shut up.

MELVIN   He's afraid of her.

TEDDY   Everyone shut the fuck up. Alright. Let's vote now. Who votes for Melvin? (*no one puts up their hand*) Who votes for me? (*TEDDY and NIGGER put up their hands*) Alright. Thank you. I accept your nomination as new Chief. I will serve you good. Amen.

***

Downsizing Democracy: A Polemic

by Mansel Robinson

A one-person theatrical lecture, complete with blackboards, newspaper clippings, adding machines, photographs, numbers, quotes, contradictions, cops, Conrad Black and Paul Martin. The overall theme is the loss of democratic choice and citizen power under the onslaught of the corporate and neo-conservative agendas: globalisation, the gutting of the social safety net, hyper-individualism and profit uber alles. *The polemicist is an amateur (in the good sense of the word) "rooting around in the town dump of the new economy," making connections between the seemingly disconnected, putting faces on the data, testing assumptions, trying our voices, discovering self-contradictions, recognising moral conundrums, and experiencing the collision of points of view.*

By the end of the evening, the room will be covered in bits of connected information: NAFTA, MAI, Linda McQuaig, Peter Gzowski, free trade, interest rates, the Bank of Canada, Antonio Gramsci ....

The POLEMICIST is quoting from text written on the blackboard:

Bill Thorsell, editor in chief, *The Globe and Mail*, October 7 1995. "Capitalism is the conduct of war by civil means. It pits group against group in a perpetual struggle for advantage that includes all the human drama you associate with great military campaigns. The productive civil war that is the marketplace provides wonderful material for journalism, a fact that became broadly understood only in the 1980s." End quote.

"The conduct of war by civil means."

"The productive civil war that is the market place..."

When I was a kid, I liked to read all night. Anytime I could get away
with it, weekends, holidays, Christmas. A stack of books and I'm up
all night. I liked it best just before the town started to wake up. A
garbage truck. A brakeman walking home after a graveyard shift in
the yard. Nurses going home, the sun coming up, their white heels
clicking on the sidewalk or crunching through the snow. I liked it that
she'd been up all night, clicking her heels through the halls, looking
in the wards, stopping at a doorway to listen to an old man breathe,
checking the preemies for colour and pulse. I felt safe knowing she'd
been up all night. Safer knowing that than listening to my own
parents breathing in the next room.

So.

I became a doctor.

Ten years in school. Residency. The Hippocratic oath: "Above all, do
no harm."

Well.

When the downsizing frenzy hit Alberta there was no room for me. Or
there was room, but the government didn't want me. Cutting programs
is not a matter of left and right it's a matter of arithmetic, etc. etc. So
I headed south. I'm still a doctor. But I haven't seen a patient in two
years. I work for a Health Management Organization, a private health
care company owned by a private health insurance company.

I sit at a desk, a nice desk, corner office, big windows. I don't see
patients. I read files. I read your file. More specifically, I read your
child's file. During a routine physical, your family doctor has noticed
a shadow on her lung. It might be nothing at all. But it might be
tuberculosis. Or lung cancer. The specialist says she needs tests,
expensive tests. A bronchoscopy, say.

But my job is not to heal the sick. My job is to protect the
sharehholder.

So I protect the shareholder.

Let's say I've already authorized my quota of bronchoscopies for the
week. If I go over quota, I'm cutting into profit.

My job is to *protect* profit. So I must deny further testing.

That's what I'm paid to do. And the sharehholder sleeps easy.

If you're lucky, and if your child is lucky, the shadow is a just scar from an old and undetected case of pneumonia. If not...

One way to eliminate skyrocketing health costs is to eliminate the patient.

You don't have to debate euthanasia. Euthanasia's here.

Bottom line.

Edmonton Journal, July 23, 1997. "Social Services Minister Lyle Oberg has just announced that the province plans to cut seven million dollars from early childhood programs for poor preschoolers." End quote.

The Globe and Mail, November 28, 1997. "Campaign 2000, the tireless antipoverty advocate has abandoned its goal for the elimination of child poverty in Canada by the end of the century and is talking up the need for sound fiscal management in furthering the interests of children. The group said that any serious social investment must not lead to a new round of deficits." End quote.

Fuck the children.

Yeah. Fuck the children.

Why should we pay taxes?

Why should we pay all those taxes for public education?

Clean water. An ozone layer. Old growth forests. Parks.

Nurses. Daycare. Music. Books. After-school sports. Museums.

Libraries.

Fuck it.
You want to keep your money in your pocket? Here's how to do it.
Demand legislation to outlaw deficit financing and the tax increases that always come with that kind of budgeting. Demand legislation

that outlaws all tax increases without a referendum — because no one is ever, ever nuts enough to vote themselves a tax increase. And if that means fuck the children — then fuck the children.

It wouldn't be the first time.

Your car's punching a hole in the ozone — you buy the kiddies sunblock.

PCB's in the water table — you invest in bottled water. The Canadian shield is a clear-cut from sea to fished-out sea? Boo hoo hoo. I've never seen a dinosaur either but that's called history. That's called progress. And don't worry. Your kids won't blame you. They'll fuck their children too.

That's called life.

The Globe and Mail, November 28, 1997. "Child poverty is up 99 percent in Ontario since 1989. Up 34 percent in Alberta. Up 59 percent overall in Canada." End quote.

OK. By now you should be asking yourself, who is this Chatty Cathy doll, somebody pulled his string — now listen to him sing. Call me a cynic but there is only one important question:

Who's paying? So by now you should be asking: Who does this Chatty Cathy doll work for? How much does he make?

What's in it for him?

Good questions. Thanks for asking. So let's follow the money. I am an economic migrant — I go where I have to go, I do what I have to do, an economic refugee. I'm freelance, entrepreneurial, self-employed and claiming every tax deduction within spitting distance of legality.

And tonight, I've been hired to help you pick your way through the battle zone of the Canadian political economy. Now I suspect some of you are wondering about the title *Downsizing Democracy*. Isn't this a little ... overstated? I mean isn't everything just peachy keen? The Alberta deficit has been eliminated. The socialist-tax-and-spend-government of Saskatchewan has tabled five balanced budgets in a row.

On February 25, 1998, *The Globe and Mail* blares: "The books are balanced! The books are balanced!" (*blowing a party whistle — toot toot toot*) Isn't that battle over? In fact, aren't all the battles over?

(*holding up a book*) This guy thinks so. Francis Fukuyama, *The End of History and the Last Man.* "Technology makes possible the limitless accumulation of wealth, and thus the satisfaction of an ever-expanding set of human desires. This process guarantees an increasing homogenization of all human societies, regardless of their historical origins or cultural inheritances. All countries undergoing economic modernization must increasingly resemble one another. They must replace traditional forms of social organization like tribe, sect and family with economically rational ones based on function and efficiency. Such societies have become increasingly linked with one another through global markets and the spread of a universal consumer culture. Moreover, the logic of modern natural science would seem to indicate a universal evolution in the direction of capitalism." End quote.

Heavy stuff, yes, but I think Mr. Fukuyama is simply saying: the human being has evolved into an efficient consumer, shopping contentedly and complacently in some well-lit, well-stocked global WalMart. We have arrived at the end of history. The last man. Woman. And child.

So. Apparently, the battle is over.

But *my* question is: which battle are we talking about? The biggest one in recent memory was the deficit battle. Remember the sniper fire from *The Globe and Mail*? (*directed at individual audience members*)

(*pointing*) You — you, you "Victim of the week".

(*pointing*) You — you, you "Chronic user of the U.I. syringe".

(*pointing*) You— you "Special-interest group".

(*pointing*) You — "Whiner"

(*pointing*) You — "Complainer".

(*pointing*) You — "NDPer".

(*pointing*) You — card-carrying member of "The loony left".

(*pointing*) You you you you "Communist".

Remember that onslaught, that strategy of personal abuse?

Remember the suffering you went through in the Blitzkrieg attack on the deficit? Lost teaching jobs? Closed hospitals? Is that the battle I'm talking about?

Well, yes and no.

Well ... no.

If the military theorist von Klauzwitz is right that war is the continuation of *politics,* by other means, then my argument tonight is extrapolated from William Thorsell's argument: economics is a continuation of war by other means. (*underlining Thorsell's phrases on the board*) So that's what interests me here tonight: economics as war by other means.

Now, I suspect some of you will want clarity — unequivocal, unambiguous, unambivalent, clarity.

But I'm afraid I have nothing to — offer but images: images of money, power, revenge, greed, murder, larceny and lies — in other words, a typically Canadian war story. But let me be perfectly clear: you have no reason to trust me. If the first casualty of war is truth, then the first casualty in the civil war called the marketplace is the truth about self-interest.

(*writing self-interest on the board*) OK. Let's connect some dots.

***

Annie Mae's Movement

by Yvette Nolan

*A two-hander that follows the life of Anna Mae Aquash, a
Micmac from Nova Scotia, from her involvement with the
American Indian Movement at Wounded Knee in 1974
through to her death in February, 1976.*

Opening Monologue

> *ANNA MAE is isolated onstage in a pool of light.
> She is wearing jeans, a light-coloured shirt, and a
> wine-coloured windbreaker. On her wrist is a
> large turquoise bracelet. She is doing karate
> moves.*

ANNA MAE

There are all kinds of ways of getting rid of people. In Central
America they disappeared people. Just came and took them away in
the middle of the night, whoosh gone, and then deny everything. Very
effective. Well, here they disappear people too. They disappear them
by keeping them underfed, keeping them poor, prone to sickness and
disease. They disappear them into jails. In jails they disappear their
dignity, their pride. Also very effective. It's easier than you might
think to disappear people in this country, especially Indian people.
Innuendo and manipulation, false evidence, lies. No due process.
Whoosh, gone. Then just deny everything.

Sometimes I worry that I am disappeared from my kids' lives, so far
away fighting for — what?

When my babies were born, I tried so hard. I read the child
psychology books — Dr. Spock, eh? — underlining the important
passages. The girls were disciplined, bed at a certain time, finish
everything on your plate, all the time explaining the reasons for the
rules...

But it's not enough anymore to have food and shelter. There's got to be more to leave my kids than that.

I'd do anything, anything to protect them. My little brother Francis, he used to get bugged something awful, and I learned to fight to protect him. I could take any boy in my class. And then, when my mother left, well, Francis was still little, only ten...

I guess I got it from my mother, she used to fight with the Indian Agent. This one time, he brought us a bunch of clothes, *donations* — army coats and what do you call those pants they wear riding horses? - all moth-eaten, full of holes. I couldn't have been more than four, but I remember she sent him packing, with his crummy rags. After that, he finally started sending us better stuff. After *that,* she'd write letters to Ottawa, to Halifax, every time he pissed her off.

She was like that, tough. Me too, I always been tough. I used to ride a pig when I was little. Big mean old thing in the barnyard, man he used to get so mad, he'd slam himself against the barn trying to get me off, but I just held on.

> *There is the sound of helicopters approaching.*
> *Wind begins to blow. The legs in the theatre flap.*
> *ANNA MAE continues to struggle at first to*
> *continue her training, then to keep her feet. She*
> *is driven to her knees. There are shouts offstage*
> *and the sound of walkie talkies. ANNA MAE*
> *escapes left.*
>
> *FBI agent runs on from right. He is in full*
> *paramilitary gear—- khakis, army boots wearing*
> *sunglasses and carrying an automatic weapon.*

AGENT   Right. Let's get this show on the road.

***

Annie Mae's Movement

by Yvette Nolan

Closing Monologue

ANNA

I started survival schools in the States. The idea was, if we could give kids the tools to live in the white world, but not let them lose their Indianness, give 'em a sense of pride in who they were, where they come from, we could help to rebuild an Indian Nation that was self-sufficient, autonomous, healthy and whole.

I started survival schools. Those who can, do. Those who can't, teach. Those who can't, can't. Don't. Don't.

> *FBI AGENT has entered and is watching her. She becomes aware of him. As he approaches her, her "don't"s become more agitated, pleading, angry, anguished. As he rapes her, she stops begging and begins to say:*

My name is Anna Mae Pictou Aquash, Micmac Nation from Shubenacadlie, Nova Scotia. My mother is Mary Ellen Pictou, my father is Francis Thomas Levi, my sisters are Rebecca Julien and Mary Lafford, my brother is Francis. My daughters are Denise and Deborah. You cannot kill us all. You can kill me, but my sisters live, my daughters live. You cannot kill us all. My sisters live. Becky and Mary, Helen and Priscilla, Janet and Raven, Sylvia, Ellen , Pelajia, Agnes, Monica, Edie, Jessica, Gloria and Lisa and Muriel, Monique, Joy and Tina, Margo, Maria, Beatrice, April, Colleen...

You can kill me, but you cannot kill us all. You can kill me.

> *FBI AGENT pulls out a handgun and shoots her behind the right ear. She falls on her left side, drawing her knees up slightly. He exits.*

***

Index of Plays

Index of Playwrights